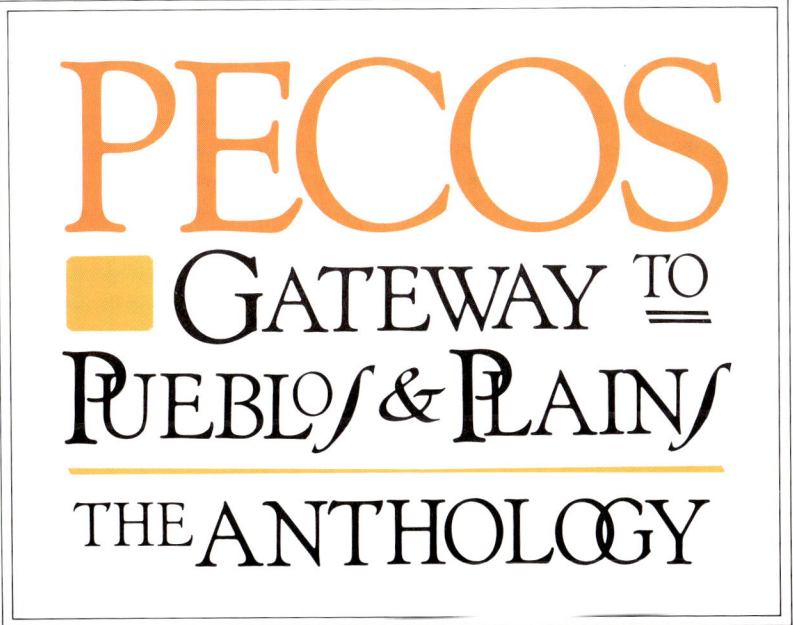

Edited by
John V. Bezy
Joseph P. Sanchez

PUBLISHED BY SOUTHWEST PARKS AND MONUMENTS ASSOCIATION
WITH ASSISTANCE FROM THE FRIENDS OF PECOS NATIONAL MONUMENT

Dedicated To

*Alfred E. Kidder who explored and documented
the history of Pecos.*

◆

*E. E. Fogelson and Greer Garson Fogelson who worked
in cooperation with the Department of the Interior
and National Park Service for the preservation
of this national treasure.*

Copyright 1988 by Southwest Parks & Monuments Association, Tucson, Arizona.

ISBN 0-911408-77-0 Softbound edition
ISBN 0-911408-78-0 Clothbound edition

Library of Congress Number 88-060561

Editorial: Rose Houk, Joseph P. Sanchez, & Ann Rasor.
Design & production: Christina Watkins.
Typography: Penny R. Smith.
Lithography: Lorraine Press, Inc., Salt Lake City, Utah.

PHOTOGRAPHY CREDITS

Frontispiece, pages 18, 23, 26, 28, 36, 39, 45, 49, 57, 62, 71, 77, 92,
93, 102, 111, 120, 143, 144, & back cover © George H.H. Huey.

Page 21 © Jerry Jacka.

Cover, pages 7, 16, 24, 30, 33, 65, 66, 74, 83, 98, 101, & 133 © David Muench.

Historic photographs courtesy the National Park Service.

Projectile points page 23 courtesy Arizona State Museum, University of Arizona.

ILLUSTRATION CREDITS

Illustrations pages 20, 27, 32, 41, 47, 53, 69, 76, 82, 91, 95, 104–105, 107, & 113,
© Roy Andersen.

Maps pages 15 & 108 by Kevin Leveque.

Paintings pages 12–13 & 86–87 by Tom Lovell courtesy of the Abell-Hanger
Foundation and of the Permian Basin Petroleum Museum, Midland, Texas,
where they are on display.

Illustrations pages 34, 61, & 72–73 by Lawrence Ormsby.

CONTENTS

STEWART UDALL
PREFACE 6

DONALD P. HODEL
INTRODUCTION 8

JOHN V. BEZY
I   THE GEOLOGY OF PECOS 14

RICHARD W. LANG
II   THE FIRST SIX MILLENIA 20

STEWART PECKHAM
III   THE EARLY PUEBLO PERIOD 26

ANN RASOR
IV   PECOS PUEBLO 32

JAMES H. GUNNERSON
V   APACHES AT PECOS 40

JOSEPH P. SANCHEZ
VI   CICUYE & THE FIRST SPANIARDS 46

JOSEPH P. SANCHEZ
VII   GASPAR CASTAÑO DE SOSA & CICUYE 52

JOSEPH P. SANCHEZ
VIII   PECOS MISSION IN THE SEVENTEENTH CENTURY 60

JOSEPH P. SANCHEZ
IX   PECOS IN THE EIGHTEENTH CENTURY 68

ELIZABETH A.H. JOHN
X   COMANCHES & PECOS 76

ALBERT H. SCHROEDER
XI   ANATOMY OF AN ABANDONMENT 82

FELIX D. ALMARÁZ, JR.
XII   PECOS UNDER THE MEXICAN EAGLE 86

MARC SIMMONS
XIII   WAYSTOP ON THE SANTA FE TRAIL 94

K. JACK BAUER
XIV   MANIFEST DESTINY PAUSES AT THE PECOS 100

BETSY SWANSON
XV   THE BATTLES OF GLORIETA PASS 106

VERNON J. GLOVER & JOHN McCALL
XVI   THE SANTA FE RAILWAY 112

RICHARD B. WOODBURY
XVII   A. V. KIDDER & PECOS 118

ALDEN C. HAYES
XVIII   COLONIAL PERIOD ARCHEOLOGY AT PECOS 128

EMIL W. HAURY
EPILOGUE 132

SUGGESTED READINGS 136

INDEX 139

ACKNOWLEDGMENTS 142

PREFACE

THE RUINS OF PECOS are a very special place. There are many remarkable historic sites in the Southwest protected and interpreted by the National Park Service, but Pecos stands by itself because this site is the setting of a continuous story of human activities covering a period of at least 7,000 years.

Indian history, fascinating episodes of Spanish history, and events involving the much more recent story of the westering of what we call the United States of America come together and interact at this national monument. Pecos stretches our minds and makes us ponder both the mysteries of the beginnings of civilization in this country and the resolution of the conflicts which occur when cultures collide.

The visible remains of the great Pecos Pueblo allow visitors to study one of the enchanting chapters of history that was "written" on these sloping hills. But this was a gateway both for the Indians and for those who came much later. Part of the appeal of Pecos is the fun one can have conjuring up the human pageants that passed this way and thoughts that crossed the minds of the men and women and children who made the transition from the buffalo plains into the mountains. One of Spain's greatest captains of her latter days, Governor Juan Bautista de Anza, came to this spot to sit down with Comanche war chiefs and arrange a peace which gave a long respite to Spaniards and Pueblo Indians in the Río Grande Valley. Where did their powwow take place? And what did the horsemen look like as they approached their appointed rendezvous? One's imagination can run wild at Pecos.

This is more than a ruin, a historic site, a landmark. The long parade of Indians and non-Indians, who came by this entrance to the important pass west from here, knew it as a campsite and a water hole, and they knew it as a place to contemplate their next adventure. Buffalo hunters, and "Comancheros" who rode by on their way to trade with the Plains Indians, as well as Spanish, Mexican and Anglo American armies who were the vanguard of settlement, and the men, women, and children who laid down the wagon tracks that became the Santa Fe Trail, all paused as they passed by here.

Pecos is a special place. Enjoy it. It invites all of us to pause and ponder where our civilization came from—and where it is going.

STEWART UDALL

INTRODUCTION

IN 1949, historian Herbert Eugene Bolton described the march of civilization through Pecos with these words:

> Pecos, "was the gateway for Pueblo Indians when they went Buffalo hunting on the Plains; a two-way pass for barter and war between Pueblos and Plains tribes; a portal through the mountains for Spanish explorers, traders, and buffalo hunters; for the St. Louis caravan traders with Santa Fe; for pioneer Anglo American settlers; for Spanish and Saxon Indian fighters; for Civil War armies; and for a transcontinental railroad passing through the Southwest."

This beautifully illustrated anthology traces the historical procession of these peoples in a series of vignettes of Pecos's past. The European encounter with Indian America took place here as it did over much of the Western Hemisphere. Forty-eight years after Columbus's landing, Francisco Vasquez de Coronado stood outside the gates of Pecos. Thus began a pattern of change that was to mold the destiny of Pecos as successive groups came to conquer, pray and trade.

PECOS: GATEWAY TO PUEBLO & PLAINS, suggests a metaphor much more encompassing than merely an early avenue of commerce. From the beginning this gateway facilitated cultural exchange among numerous groups. In the twentieth century, it has been a focus for southwestern archeology and history. After archeologically exploring Pecos, A. V. Kidder developed a system for classifying pottery which unlocked the prehistory of the American Southwest. Today, as a national monument, Pecos remains a gateway that beckons the modern visitor to explore the rich Native American, Hispanic, and Anglo heritage of this national treasure.

Although this publication is dedicated to those who shaped Pecos history, I would like to make a special dedication to Colonel E. E. and Mrs. Greer Garson Fogelson, whose generosity and commitment preserved this history. To them, we are indebted.

With careers spanning the worlds of theatre, film, business and education, Greer Garson is recognized internationally for artistic excellence and popularity in British and American theatre and films.

Her Viking, Scottish and Irish ancestry undoubtedly supplied the determination she needed to pursue a stage career despite many obstacles. Educated at the University of London and the University of Grenoble, she dreamed of working in the theatre and, after a start at the Birmingham Repertory Theatre, soon became the toast of London's West End. A three-year marathon of starring in spirited and romantic roles in London plays was interrupted when Louis B. Mayer of M.G.M. Studios persuaded her to come with her widowed mother to America and embark upon a career in motion pictures.

Along with her beauty and talent, she brought a gentle dignity to the screen, a quality that endeared her to movie-goers of all ages. Her twenty-five films include *Goodbye Mr. Chips, Pride and Prejudice, Blossoms in the Dust, Random Harvest, Madame Curie, Mrs. Parkington, Valley of Decision,* and *Mrs. Miniver*—a gallery of inspiring characters that earned her seven Academy

Mrs. Greer Garson Fogelson

nominations including the coveted Oscar.

Her marriage in 1949 to Colonel E. E. Fogelson of Dallas added new dimensions to an already legendary public life. Dividing her time between Los Angeles, Dallas, and their historic Forked Lightning Ranch at Pecos, New Mexico, she has, through the years, taken a leading role in civic and benevolent causes at the national, state, and local levels. In the field of education, she supports the Greer Garson Theatre and its scholarship and guest artist programs at The College of Santa Fe, and similar enterprises at various other universities. She is currently working on her latest project, the creation of a Film and Television Center at The College of Santa Fe.

E. E. Fogelson—soldier, lawyer, geologist, and pioneer oil producer—was born in Nebraska of Finnish immigrants. His father was a college teacher of philosophy and languages, and his parents' respect for learning is reflected in Buddy Fogelson's academic training. He is an alumnus of Nebraska and Texas Christian universities, a member of the State Bar of Texas and the Southwest Legal Foundation, and a Fellow of Boston University.

During World War II he was assigned to General Dwight D. Eisenhower's staff and awarded numerous military citations, including the Croix de Guerre avec Palme twice, from the French Government. After the war, President Truman appointed Colonel Fogelson as a member of the American Delegation to the Allied Reparations Commission at Moscow.

His life's work has involved the search for oil, gas

and minerals. His spare time, energies, and philanthropic involvement have been directed largely toward the education of young people, as witnessed by his long tenure as a National Director of the Boy's Clubs of America, and the Fogelson Library Center at The College of Santa Fe. For decades he has contributed generously to the building of new facilities and to scholarship funds at various universities, making a college degree financially possible for hundreds of young people.

His civic involvements, particularly in realms of art, opera, and theatre, have included serving as president of the Dallas Little Theatre; as a former Director of the Santa Fe Opera; and as an active supporter of the Metropolitan Opera Company in Dallas. He has endowed various hospitals and medical research endeavors, and has for years been a director on the Board of the Eisenhower Medical Center at Indian Wells, California.

Greer and Buddy Fogelson share a common love for the natural and cultural heritage of the Pecos Valley. Unquestionably, much of the rare historical and archeological treasure of the Pecos Valley is preserved today because of their tireless efforts.

In June 1965, the pueblo and mission of Pecos were designated as a national monument, culminating a thirty-year effort by the Fogelsons to obtain Federal protection for the site. In 1964, they donated 279 acres from their Forked Lightning Ranch to form a buffer zone around the original sixty-two acres of the ruins. This zone excludes any commercial activity in the area,

Colonel E. E. Fogelson

and benefits each visitor who walks the ruins trail and experiences being part of this historic and natural scene.

Fifteen years later they donated an additional twenty-three acres including the Forked Lightning Ruin, which dates back to A.D. 1150 and is a vital link in the occupational chain of the Pecos Valley. In 1981 their hard work and generosity were finally recognized when they were awarded the Conservation Service Award—the highest honor bestowed by the Department of the Interior.

The Fogelsons had long dreamed of building a visitor center and museum at the site of the ruins on their ranch. The Department of the Interior under President Ronald Reagan's administration welcomed the idea as an opportunity for Government and private citizens to cooperate in a civic project, and in 1984 Secretary William Clark dedicated the E. E. Fogelson Visitor Center, which provides an interpretive facility that will be enjoyed for countless generations to come. To paraphrase President Reagan, the role of Greer and Colonel Fogelson in the establishment of Pecos National Monument in 1965 and in their donation of funds, land, and key ruins, is a permanent and vital part of the Monument's history.

DONALD P. HODEL

In December of 1987, as this book was being prepared for press, Colonel E. E. Fogelson passed away in Dallas, Texas. His monumental contributions to public life, and to the preservation of Pecos National Monument, have left an indelible mark.

Sixteenth century trade fair at the pueblo of Pecos. "Overnight, the open grassy valley that spead out to the east . . . was transformed into an Apache rendezvous with clusters of conical skin tipis, running children, yapping dogs, and the smoke of a hundred fires." John Kessell, Kiva, Cross and Crown.

I THE GEOLOGY OF PECOS • JOHN V. BEZY

Geologic Circumstance &

geographic location have made Pecos a cultural crossroad for centuries. Human activities here have centered around the Glorieta-Pecos corridor, a thirty-mile-long natural passage eroded between the Sangre de Cristo Range and Glorieta Mesa by mountain streams. The high middle section of this corridor is Glorieta Pass. Since prehistoric times, travel and commerce between people of the upper Rio Grande Valley and the Great Plains have funneled through this strategic portal.

Three great geologic provinces join in the vicinity of Pecos. To the north and east, the Rocky Mountains reach their southernmost extension in the Sangre de Cristo Range. The parallel mountains and intervening basins of the Basin and Range province begin on the south and west at Glorieta Mesa and the Río Grande Depression and continue south into central Mexico. To the east are the Great Plains, stretching for nearly 900 unbroken miles to the Mississippi River. The Glorieta-Pecos corridor is a gateway of continental significance.

Geologically, the story of the Pecos area began 290 million years ago during the Pennsylvanian Period. At that time, the sea repeatedly advanced and retreated across this region, depositing limy ooze, mud, and sand. Over time, these deposits became compacted and cemented into the hard, erosion-resistant limestones and sandstones that are exposed in the cliffs and canyons north and east of the national monument. It is through these beds that the Pecos River has cut its narrow, north-south canyon.

A younger and completely different sequence of rocks is encountered in the vicinity of the village of Pecos, where the river exits the canyon. Here, in the Tecolote Range (a low spur of the Sangre de Cristo Mountains) and at Glorieta Mesa are exposed the soft shales and sandstones of the Sangre de Cristo Formation. These red and maroon sedimentary rocks are less resistant to erosion than either the older Pennsylvanian rocks to the north and east or the younger Permian strata in the walls of Glorieta Mesa, and their weakness offered a natural avenue along which the Pecos River could cut a valley draining onto the Great Plains.

Geological structure also played a role in creating

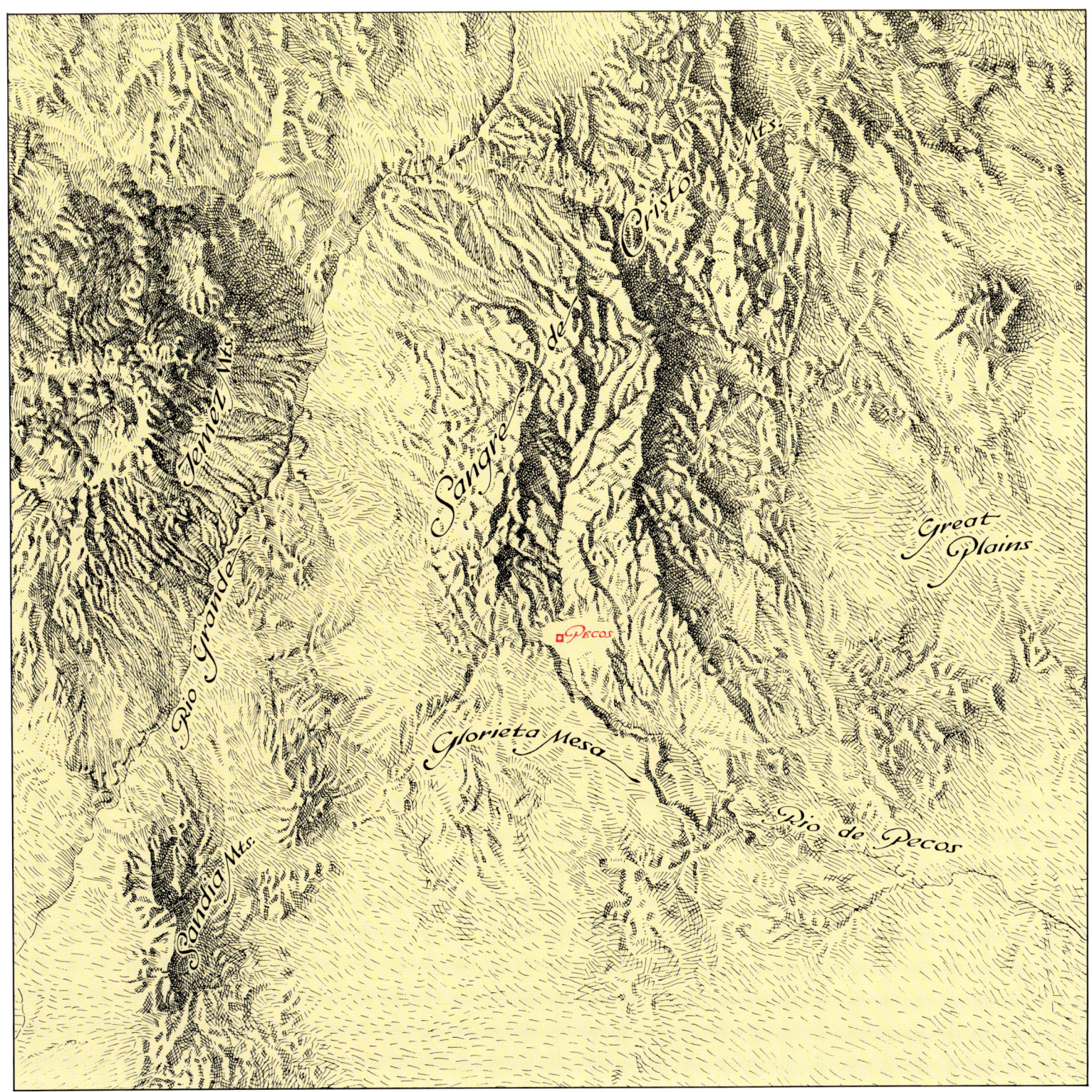

THE GEOLOGY OF PECOS

They constructed pueblo walls with sandstone blocks from the mesilla and igneous and metamorphic cobbles carried from nearby terraces and Glorieta Creek.

the present topography. The Tecolote Range, east of Pecos Monument, is formed by an archlike fold in erosion-resistant Pennsylvanian and Permian limestones. The Pecos River, following the path of least resistance, swung around these mountains and the southward-dipping beds that make up Glorieta Mesa. Thus confined, the river excavated the broad lowland in which the pueblo was built and that is now followed by Interstate 25 and the Santa Fe Railroad. Similar erosion of the same formation by Glorieta and Galisteo creeks has formed the western half of the Glorieta-Pecos corridor. Subsequent uplift of the land and downcutting by streams have shifted the Pecos River eastward to its present entrenched course along the western flanks of the Tecolote Range. High terraces and deep alluvial deposits containing cobbles of micaceous schist, granite, diorite, and quartzite today mark the former course of the river.

Weathering and erosion have since modified the topography of the valley. Streams are rapidly cutting into the old terrace surfaces and exposing the bedrock below. In fact, the mission-pueblo ruins at the monument are built on a sandstone and shale ridge being exhumed from the alluvial fill. This site provided a number of environmental advantages. Here the pueblo enjoyed the solar heating of southerly exposure and avoided cold air drainage from Pecos Canyon. Water was available at a small spring east of the mesilla (small mesa) and from Glorieta Creek. From the pueblo, farmers had easy access to the alluvial bottomlands along the Pecos River and Glorieta Creek, as well as their dry-farmed plots on nearby terraces. Strategically the site gave unobstructed views and adequate warning of enemy approach and provided control of trade and travel through the Glorieta-Pecos corridor. In times of warfare, the mesilla became a natural fortress.

Lower terraces, inset into the much older Pecos River terrace deposits, record more recent episodes of downcutting along the river's course. Indian and Hispanic settlers alike sought out these flat surfaces for village sites and agricultural fields.

Technologically a Stone Age people, the pueblo inhabitants of the Pecos Valley depended heavily on the unusual variety of nearby rock resources. They constructed pueblo walls with sandstone blocks from the mesilla and igneous and metamorphic cobbles carried from nearby terraces and Glorieta Creek. Schists and quartzites from the latter groups were used as hammerstones, or made into pot polishers, arrow shaft straighteners, smoking pipes, and ceremonial objects.

Other materials used by Native Americans and Hispanics came from greater distances. Translucent selenite used for windows and other forms of gypsum used for plaster were quarried from the slopes of Glorieta Mesa; mica sheets from near Cowles were made into ornamental discs. By virtue of its gateway location, numerous items, such as petrified wood, lignite, flint, turquoise, fibrolite axheads, salt, obsidian, and shell came to the area through trade.

Changes in the land have also occurred during historic times, perhaps as a consequence of Hispanic and Anglo overgrazing and timbering. When Father Domínguez visited Pecos Pueblo in 1776, he described

THE GEOLOGY OF PECOS

nearby Glorieta Creek as "a very good river of good water and many delicious trout." Since that visit, this and other streams in the region have entrenched their channels through former valley floors, forming steep-walled, flat-bottomed drainages, called "arroyos" in the Southwest. Whatever the cause, accelerated erosion by these drainages has destroyed large areas once used for agriculture and grazing.

Large-scale exploitation of industrial and precious minerals came with Anglo settlement. Zinc, lead, copper, silver, and gold were mined from 1925 to 1939 at Terrero, fourteen miles up Pecos Canyon. These minerals were exported from the region, and except for tailings left near the village of Pecos, mining has had no lasting impact on the area.

Today, a modern interstate highway is within easy view of the ruined pueblo and church. Together, these structures span centuries of southwest history as testament to the role of geology and geographical location in the human experience.

The Pecos River shaped the character of the valley over the centuries and brought life to the people who settled there.

PECOS

9000 B.C.
·
A.D. 1500

II THE FIRST SIX MILLENNIA · RICHARD W. LANG

AT LEAST 11,000 YEARS AGO

on the fringes of the Pecos country nomadic hunters began roving when the prevailing climate was both wetter and colder than today. These Paleo-Indians of the Llano, Folsom, and Plano cultures thinly occupied what is now northern New Mexico until about 6000 B.C. Their tool caches and hunting sites occasionally have been found as close to the upper Pecos as the Las Vegas Plateau, the juniper-edged prairies and foothills near Santa Fe, and the eastern highlands of the Galisteo Basin.

Certainly these ancient hunters would have known of the Pecos Valley and must have realized that the river that flowed east and south into the sage-grasslands where they pursued the Columbian mammoth, bison, horse, and camel had its source in the distant, snowy mountains. But, if they journeyed through the valley, we have yet to discover any positive evidence of their passing.

These were people of the grasslands, adapted to hunting large, herding and grazing mammals; the dank, forested Pecos Valley and treeless tundra that loomed above it probably offered the Paleo-Indians few attractions. Even when, after 8600 B.C., the great cold waned, the valley remained forest and woodlands. As the Southwest began to dry out, the last big-game hunters withdrew to the Great Plains.

In doing so, they made way for other people of a distinctly different life style—the Western Archaic—who had been evolving for thousands of years in the coastal chaparral, savannas, and deserts of the far West. There, the key to survival lay in subsistence versatility. In the harshest ranges of these lands few animals would have been rejected as food sources.

Under the warmer, drier climate that followed the end of the last Ice Age, desert scrubland and chaparral reclaimed much of the Southwest. The Archaic people now saw the opening of enormous new territories to which their culture was preadapted. Their range expanded with that of the arid lands and by the fifth millenium B.C. their descendants had wandered into what is today New Mexico.

Their appearance in the Pecos area, between about 5500 and 4800 B.C., ushers in the long Archaic epoch which was to last, as a basic stage of cultural adaptation,

To the archaic people the great expanses of sky and earth was home. This vast land provided all the necessities of life—food, game, and the material for their tools.

until A.D. 400–500. It was an age without permanent housing, a time when life was lived in small groups, an epoch of purposeful and almost continuous movement in search of food and necessary raw materials. Men and women developed an all-important and intimate understanding of the natural world; during the Archaic significant and fundamental achievements—conceptual, technological, economic and social—were gained. The essential foundation was laid for the eventual rise of the more complex and elaborate farming societies we call Anasazi, Mogollon, and Pueblo.

Both tools and campsites of earliest Archaic man in Pecos show a folk whose energies were strongly focused upon the hunt. Group safety and human survival seem to have hung primarily upon the merits of the hunter. He would have had an extensive body of knowledge and skill that extended well beyond making and using essential tools like the compound dart and spear-thrower or atlatl. The atlatl was a remarkable device that extended the length of the hunter's arm by about two feet and increased both the power of thrust and the distance at which game might be hit. Such knowledge had to include a thorough understanding of the habits of the animals hunted—crucial information by which hare, rabbit, squirrel, deer, elk, or bighorn sheep might be brought to ground. The Archaic hunter was undoubtedly an extraordinary tracker and stalker, capable of tremendous stamina and persistence in the chase.

Between about 4800 and 3200 B.C., Archaic people became engaged in a more extensive and intensive exploitation of the environment, employing special tools to enhance the effectiveness and efficiency of the food quest. Principal among these were those hallmark artifacts of the seed gleaner, the grinding slab and hand stone, or mano. These milling tools, used to grind seed to flour or a buttery paste, became abundant by about 3300 B.C. They heralded a fundamental economic change of enormous proportions. Seeds furnished by a wide variety of plants, including grasses, offered a relatively dependable source of food during summer and autumn. Rich in calories, these seeds would store over several months, increasing the possibility of human survival during the barren seasons of winter and early spring. The increased focus on seed collection firmed the Archaic people's grip upon existence. Too, it surely must have elevated the role of women, the principal food collectors in hunting-gathering societies, to new prominence.

After about 3200 to 1800 B.C., Archaic populations were growing and the people were becoming classic foragers. Much evidence indicates that these people were tied to a seasonal life style synchronized with plant and animal cycles, scarcity or abundance, and that they commonly moved from one resource locale to the next as small, independent, family groups. Their material goods were mostly lightweight and highly portable. The inventory known from dry caves in the Southwest is starkly utilitarian—weapons, knives, scrapers, drills and perforators, snares, nets, digging sticks used to uncover and dislodge bulbs and tubers, rope and cordage, hides, pouches, finger-woven textile bags and carrying bands, cradles for toting infants, sandals, caps and cool weather robes of fur-wrapped string, wooden scoops, and a variety

The large flinted projectile point of the Paleo-Indian contrasts with the smaller points of Archaic-people who hunted smaller game.

of baskets used in cooking, storage, and transport. Heavier tools, such as those used in seed processing, were often cached at regularly visited places, ready for use. Religious articles were simple and jewelry rare.

Drought and winter were their greatest enemies, and their best shield against catastrophe was a close knowledge of the land over which they passed: of fruiting and seeding times, of the places where deer would congregate, where the large-seeded ricegrass grew thickly, of individual patterns and preferences of many plants and animals, and of the basic yearly influence of temperature, moisture, and wind upon them. Late winter and spring surely marked difficult times, when food stores might be depleted or exhausted. The specter of starvation would haunt them in these seasons when foraging possibilities were minimal. In good years, the bounties of the land increased dramatically with the coming of summer. Fall marked the end of the gathering year, culminating in the collection of cactus fruit, amaranth and sunflower seeds, acorns, and calorie-rich pine nuts so important to winter food stores. Some Archaic sites of the woodland zone showing several, fairly evenly spaced hearths may represent multifamily camping places associated with the nut harvest.

Considering the greater severity of winter at elevations above 6,000 feet, much of the upper Pecos may have been vacated in favor of lower elevation camps near water and firewood. Here, caves or rock overhangs might provide shelter, or small, simple huts could be built quickly or repaired. It is possible that winter gatherings of several family groups were occurring by

THE FIRST SIX MILLENIA

*S*eeds furnished by a wide variety of plants, including grasses, offered a relatively dependable
source of food during summer and autumn.

about 1800 to 800 B.C., these normally isolated people waiting out the long cold in some degree of mutual support and sociality. Also from this period comes the earliest evidence for corn growing in the northern Río Grande.

Domesticated much earlier in Mexico, corn and its cultivation is believed to have diffused north into the Southwest by perhaps 2000 B.C. Initially, corn growing is unlikely to have had major impact on the Archaic people. It would have provided one more crop among the many wild crops harvested during the year. However, with the later addition of beans and squash, cultivated crops gained importance. Ripening in late summer and autumn, these crops added greatly to the quantity and nutritional value of winter food stores. Evidence from the upper Pecos suggests a significant growth in population during this period, and as population and social complexity grew, greater reliance was placed upon agriculture. Ultimately, cultivated crops ranked as the most decisive determinant of the economy, the seasonal cycle, and the course of demographic and cultural change.

By about 100 B.C. to A.D. 400, which marks the beginning of the Anasazi sequence, population increase appears to have reached particularly dramatic levels in the Pecos country and the greater region. Bridging the older Archaic lifeways and the more sedentary and strongly agricultural adaptations of the Basketmaker III period, these people must have borne much of the cultural stress of that transition. Stresses may have included unprecedented pressures on resources and territory, which forced Basketmaker II colonists eastward beyond Pecos into the valley of the Canadian River. By the fifth or sixth century A.D., dispersed villages containing larger populations appeared along the Río Grande. The existence of a formative priesthood and an elaborated ceremonialism is suggested; long-distance trade had become more common; the bow and arrow had largely, if not wholly, replaced the atlatl and dart; pottery of Mogollon and early Anasazi style was being made; and farming had become central to all activities. With these events, the great Archaic epoch closed and an utterly new way of life emerged.

III THE EARLY PUEBLO PERIOD
STEWART PECKHAM

BETWEEN A.D. 300 & 1300 the Four Corners area of New Mexico, Colorado, Utah, and Arizona was inhabited by Indians called Anasazi. Their earliest settlements consisted of semi-subterranean dwellings (pithouses), but by A.D. 900 the Anasazi were living in multiroom, masonry pueblos. Associated with these pueblos were underground ceremonial rooms (kivas). The Anasazi were farmers—growing corn, beans, and squash—and potters—making black-on-white or gray vessels for everyday or ceremonial use. Eventually, these people would be a strong influence on the Pecos Valley.

The Pecos area had great potential to provide people with food, shelter, water, and raw materials. These were very likely the attractions that led family-sized groups of early farming Indians to establish permanent pithouses within a spear's throw of the mesilla, or small tableland, that 400 years later would provide the solid footing for the early clustered rooms of Pecos Pueblo. They may have been descendants of local Archaic people who lived at the southern end of the Sangre de Cristo Mountains and out onto nearby prairies. Because they farmed, built permanent dwellings, and made simple pottery, they may have been in contact with Anasazi living west of the Río Grande. In adopting Anasazi ways, these pithouse dwellers may have been among the earliest of the Río Grande Anasazi

Fourteenth century Biscuit A Bowl. A "peculiar, soft, light colored" pottery made in the Río Grande Valley and traded to the Pecos.

THE EARLY PUEBLO PERIOD

to occupy this part of the Pecos Valley.

A pithouse recently excavated at Pecos National Monument exemplifies the prevailing architectural style of the time. The large, somewhat rounded rectangular dwelling was shallowly dug into the hard natural soil. Its walls and roof were constructed of logs and poles, thatched with brush and tree bark, and plastered with mud to form a dome-shaped structure that was high enough for a ground-level doorway.

In the center of the room a basin-shaped pit served as a hearth and was probably located directly beneath a smoke hole in the roof. A low wall of mud and poles built between the hearth and door deflected any draft that would have blown over the fire. Also near the hearth was a shallow pit filled with rocks which, when heated, would have provided a long-lasting warmth for the room. Other low walls divided parts of the perimeter of the room into a series of bins for storage or other specialized functions. Elsewhere, storage pits had been dug into the floor.

The remaining floor space was found littered with smashed pottery vessels—large and small jars and canteenlike vessels for water storage. Curiously, no bowls or large-mouth vessels were found. Grinding tools, debris from the manufacture of chipped stone tools, and numerous bone beads were also found, all indicating that the house had burned, causing its occupants to leave precious belongings behind as they fled for their lives. Assuming that the fire was caused by a spark from the hearth that lodged in the roof, we may also assume that the season was between late fall and early spring when

Traded from far to the south, macaw feathers were used as bright decorations in ceremonies.

an indoor fire for light and warmth would have been a necessity. Charcoal specimens date the construction of the dwelling at about A.D. 850.

But the ninth-century pithouses at Pecos seemed to have been only a brief experiment. The Pecos mesilla and the rest of the upper Pecos Valley appear to have been devoid of permanent population until the thirteenth century.

By the early 1100s, large communities near Santa Fe and Taos began to show a trend toward the multiroom, multistoried pueblo. This development may be linked to the Anasazi's increasing reliance on farming, their ability to produce greater quantities of food, and the need to construct more rooms for storing surplus food. Improved nutrition frequently encourages population growth, and this could have led to establishment of a more complex social organization than had existed during the pithouse period when the family was the principal social unit.

During this same time, small dwelling clusters began to be constructed on the bluffs overlooking Galisteo Creek, about ten miles southwest of Pecos. Their occupants may have been family groups who moved away from the increasingly populous settlements near Santa Fe and the nearby Tesuque Valley, thereby taking advantage of an adequate water supply and arable land near present-day Lamy. This area was essentially a strategic western gateway to the plains of eastern New Mexico, and from this point the Río Grande Anasazi may have made short excursions into the Pecos Valley to test its suitability for settlement.

By the middle or late twelfth century, a few Río Grande Anasazi families had built dwellings in the Pecos Valley, near the modern communities of Rivera and Villanueva, suggesting that Anasazi settlers may have bypassed the immediate vicinity of Pecos where no settlements of this period are known to occur.

Beginning in the 1100s, the Río Grande Anasazi witnessed the arrival of migrant Anasazi who had abandoned their increasingly arid and overcrowded Four Corners homeland in favor of the large amounts of moderately well-watered arable land in the Río Grande region. What had begun as a trickle increased to a flood, and by 1300 virtually all of the Four Corners Anasazi had forsaken their former lands. This resulted in the rapid filling up of all available lands in the Río Grande region, first around the flanks of the Pajarito Plateau west of the Río Grande, and then to the uplands, mesas, and valleys of the western foothills of the Sangre de Cristo Mountains. Wherever a running stream emerged from the mountains in these areas, new and larger villages were being established, some with 100 to 200 rooms. Where pressures to get shelter were great, arriving migrants even constructed small, shallow, oval pithouses, but these were abandoned as soon as more solidly built masonry dwellings were completed.

As competition for land and water increased, the Pecos Valley may have been sought as a pressure valve to relieve the Río Grande region of this huge population influx. Migrants established villages at the familiar sites we know today only by their ruins: Pecos, Forked Lightning, Rowe, Dick's, and lesser ruins. A large pueblo was established at Tecolote, ten miles south of Las Vegas,

THE EARLY PUEBLO PERIOD

The first of the colorful Glaze wares found their way to the Pecos valley by 1375. This Glaze I Red Olla probably held precious water for a pueblo family.

New Mexico, at the eastern end of the pass through the mountains, and one group of venturesome migrants went even farther east and briefly settled in small villages near the town of Watrous, almost twenty miles northeast of Las Vegas.

This was obviously a period of great unrest and resettlement. One can imagine that claims for land and water sometimes led to serious conflict. Some lives were certainly lost as villages were attacked and set afire. Some settlements were abandoned; at others, the Anasazi rebuilt and asserted their claims to the resources of the area. This scenario seems to have occurred in the Pecos area at Forked Lightning Pueblo. Vulnerable to attack in its lowland situation, its occupants appear to have joined people already living on the Pecos mesilla, and survivors from other Pecos area pueblos may have done likewise. The identities of the attackers may never be known—perhaps they were warrior raiders from other pueblos seeking to capture booty, other Anasazi attempting to settle in the area, or Caddoan-speaking Indians from the plains raiding the more affluent pueblos.

Archeologists call this stressful time the Coalition Period (circa A.D. 1150 or 1200 to 1325), during which many large villages were established and abandoned, while others grew in size and power as refugees from throughout the Río Grande region moved and coalesced into fewer and fewer major pueblos. The beginnings of almost all the modern Río Grande pueblos—and Pecos, as well—can be traced to this time. During this time also, the Anasazi became acquainted with their adopted homeland the hard way. Materials for tools and construction were sought and found; farming techniques were developed; new pottery forms, pigments, and decorative styles were introduced; Pecos became a center to which Pueblo and Plains Indians came to trade; the warriors of Pecos gained the fear and respect of all Indians of the region: and new religious concepts and rituals brought stability to the people of Pecos for the next 200 years.

IV

PECOS PUEBLO • ANN RASOR

THE GREAT PECOS PUEBLO

"a city sightly and strong," commanded the attention of traveler and trader for more than 300 years. When Spanish explorers saw Pecos in 1540, the pueblo, with 2,000 inhabitants, was at the peak of its growth and power and had been a dominant force in northern New Mexico for a century.

No one knows what the people called their village. After abandonment the Pecos descendants called it k'ak'ora—"place down where the stone is on top." Its first historic name, Cicuique or Cicuye, may have been a Spanish mispronunciation of a Tiwa word for the village—*tshiquite* or *tziquite*. "Pecos" comes from the Keresan Indian word *pe'kush* and appears in Spanish records by the late 1500s.

The Pueblo people of Pecos were very much like others of their culture living throughout the valleys and mesas of the Southwest. They were a product of their environment; a farming people dependent on summer rains to nourish their crops of corn, beans and squash; a religious people seeking comfort and harmony through an organized religious structure and calendar; and a highly organized, community-spirited people among whom individuality was less important than the welfare of the whole society. The Pecos, however, may have been a bit more cosmopolitan than many of their Pueblo cousins. Contact with the Plains Indians gave them access to new beliefs and materials that they incorporated into their lives. And since trade was an important part of their economy, it is certain that many Pecos spoke other Indian languages and had visited a large part of the Pueblo world.

But above all, the Pecos were farmers. Generations of living in their mountain valley had taught them how to coax nature into feeding a large population. The valley provided them with hundreds of acres of flat land for cultivation and three year-round sources of water. Because rainfall was unpredictable, some crops were planted among streams and washes where water would be plentiful. Crops planted on higher ground were left to the whims of the weather. At 7,000 feet, unexpected late spring and early fall frosts could wreak havoc on the crops, so seeds were planted throughout the spring to make sure not all plants would be lost. Wild plants

Pecos, ". . . lying low on its red rock ledges, half-surrounded by a crown of fir clad mountains . . ." was surely chosen as a home not only for its available water and land but for the superb surroundings. Quote by Willa Cather, *Death Comes to the Archbishop*.

PECOS PUEBLO

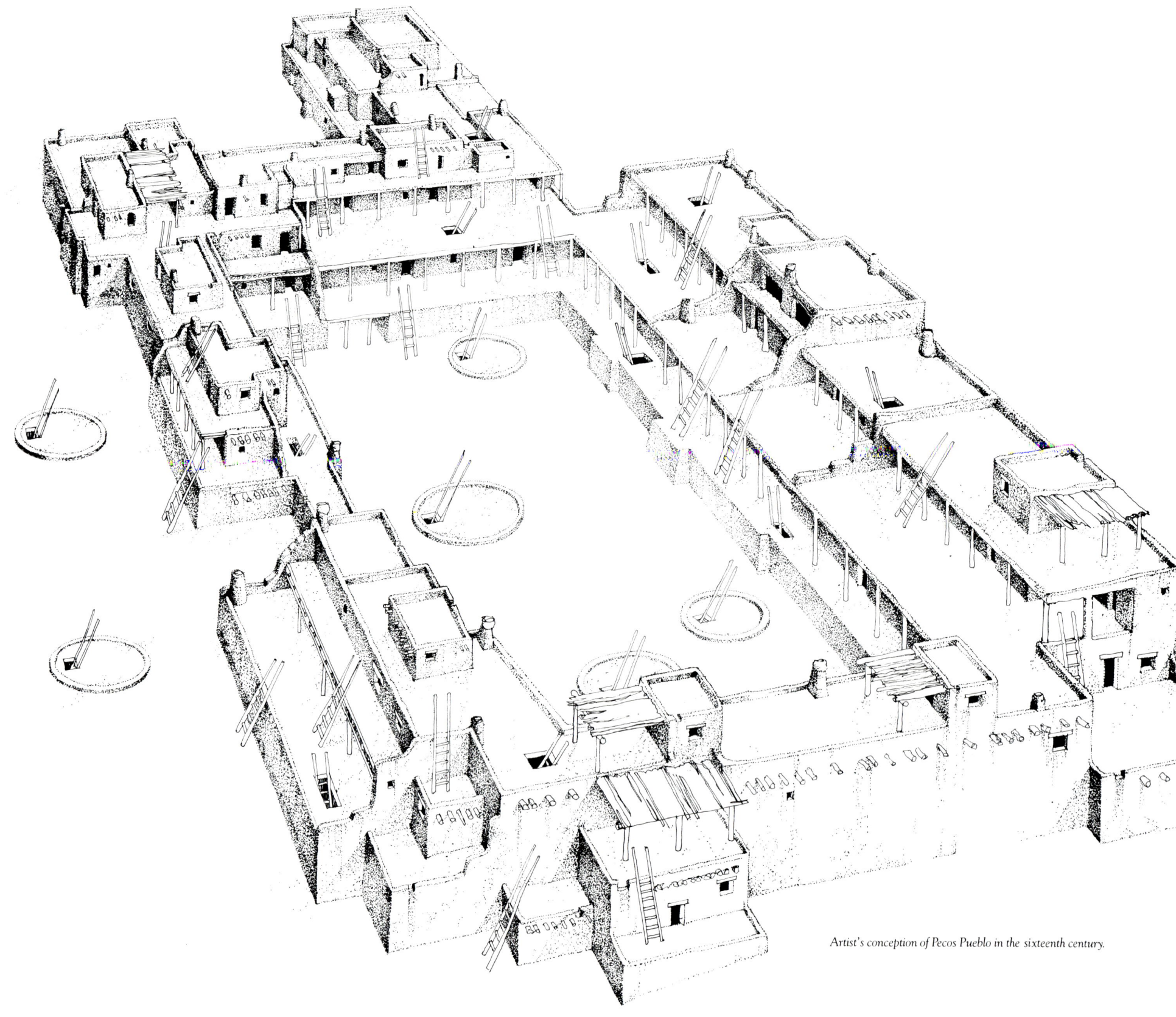

Artist's conception of Pecos Pueblo in the sixteenth century.

flourishing all over the valley provided food and healing medicines. They hunted deer, elk, antelope, buffalo, and small mammals to supplement their diet and to provide materials for tools and clothing.

To maintain harmony with the natural world the Pecos centered their lives around a strict religious calendar. Ceremonies were held throughout the year to insure a successful hunt or harvest, to bring rain to growing plants, to cure the sick, and perhaps, to bring the sun back north each year for the return of long, warm days.

Few details of Pecos social organization have survived, but they probably organized themselves into extended family groups and clans. Clan names that survived with the Pecos descendants included Cloud, Sun, Eagle, Corn, Bear, Mountain Lion, Squash, Sand, Elk, Antelope, Wild Turkey, and Fire. Clan affiliation may have determined membership in the different religious societies and leadership in the village. Leadership responsibilities were divided between the village chief (in Spanish, *cacique*), who was the spiritual and ceremonial head, and the War Priest or Chief, who protected the village from external and internal enemies. Under the War Priest were War Captains who directed secular functions including organizing people for work projects. Work was divided among all members of the pueblo. Food preparation, house repair and replastering, and pottery making were primarily women's tasks while the men were responsible for planting, hunting, room construction, and much of the weaving. Children were reared under the watchful eyes of the entire extended family. Everyone participated in building projects, irrigation canal maintenance, firewood collecting, and clearing of farmland.

Trade gave Pecos the distinction it achieved. Situated at the narrow pass through the mountains where goods and their traders must travel, the pueblo benefited as "middleman" in this active barter. Through this "corridor to other worlds" flowed items needed by both pueblo farmer and plains nomad. From the Plains Indians came slaves, buffalo hides, tallow for light, soft tanned skins for moccasins and clothing, hard flint for tools and weapons, and shell for jewelry and decoration. In turn, Plains people received fine cotton clothing, durable pottery, obsidian for sharp tools, decorative turquoise and shell, brightly colored feathers for personal and ceremonial use, and, perhaps most important, crops which a nomadic people did not usually grow.

Pecos was a military power, too. Early Spanish accounts related that "no one has been able to subdue them while they subdue what pueblos they will." During the 1400s, the Pecos extended their influence beyond the valley to control the pueblos of the Galisteo Basin to the southwest. After the Spaniards settled in New Mexico, they turned to Pecos warriors for assistance in fighting rebel Plains and Pueblo groups.

The size of Pecos impressed all who saw it. One of them, Spaniard Baltazar de Obregón, wrote in 1584 that

> Pecos is congregated on a high and narrow hill and enclosed on both sides by two streams and many trees. It has the greatest and best buildings of these provinces and is most thickly settled. It is enclosed

PECOS PUEBLO

Piñon pine and Juniper forest surrounded Pecos Pueblo. Firewood, building materials, and a wide variety of plants and animals for food, clothing and medicines were all available to the Pueblo people.

and protected by a wall and by tiers of walkways which look out on the countryside . . .

Pecos Pueblo reflected the life style and character of its people. By gathering their homes together on a rocky ridge, more land was available for farming. More important, its trade economy and frontier location dictated an elevated site from which approaching visitors could be observed. The main pueblo, built much like a fortress, reached four to five stories high. A central courtyard nestled within a protective quadrangle of apartments. The absence of windows on the outside lower stories and the presence of only two entrances into the courtyard—through narrow, winding corridors—enhanced the pueblo's formidable appearance. Ground-floor rooms had thick walls to support the stories above. Small and dark, they served for food storage or trash disposal. "Apartment living" began on the second story. Living quarters consisted of suites of rooms (usually six) occupied by an extended family. Fronting each story were porches that served as walkways around the pueblo and shady, well ventilated work space. "One can walk over the whole village without there being a street to hinder" observed an early Spanish visitor. Scattered throughout the pueblo were many kivas (sixteen reported in 1591). These round, underground rooms were reserved primarily for ceremonies. The many loom holders found in Pecos kivas indicate they also served as workrooms. Many kivas fell into disrepair and were abandoned while others were carefully remodeled. Some kivas at Pecos were in use for more than 200 years.

Local materials were the building blocks of Pecos Pueblo. Unshaped rocks, held together with mud mortar, and often post-reinforced, formed its walls. Covered with plaster to make them smooth, the stone walls required constant repair and care. Some rooms showed evidence of fifty coats of plaster. Piñon, ponderosa pine, and juniper, growing abundantly nearby, were used for roof beams and porch supports—all cut with stone axes.

A stone wall encircled the pueblo. No more than four feet high, it was not primarily for defense. Instead, it served as a boundary line to keep visitors at acceptable distances.

When archeologist A. V. Kidder started his landmark excavations of the Pecos Pueblo in the early part of this century, he encountered surprising architectural complexity. The fortress pueblo described by the Spaniards was the final form of a community that had taken shape in four different phases over more than a century. The earliest pueblo, which he called Black-on-White House, was the first village built on the small ridge or mesilla (about A.D. 1300) and contained no more than 100 rooms. Another separate small pueblo was built on the east edge of the mesilla around 1375. About 1400, the great Pecos quadrangle (the North Pueblo) began to take shape. But there was one major difference between it and its predecessors—planning. From the symmetry of architecture, wall abutments, and datable potsherds in the fill, Kidder determined that the final structure was designed and built as a unit. Apparently it resulted from a need for more organized housing as other people emigrated to the mesilla about 1400 after abandoning surrounding smaller villages. Around the time of Spanish contact, rooms were added to the south along with a series of covered portals or porches.

Kidder found evidence of small communities sharing the mesa with North Pueblo. One called 700 Pueblo was located very close to the main pueblo and seemed to have been occupied at the same time. It may have housed 300 people. South Pueblo, the community at the southern end of the mesilla near the mission, remains a mystery. It probably did not reach its largest size until well into the historic period and may have evolved as a community of Indians more loyal to the mission.

During the centuries that generations of people lived at Pecos, much of their broken pottery, worn utensils, food scraps, and other debris were thrown over the eastern edge of the mesilla. More than a quarter mile long, and twenty feet deep in places, this trash mound proved to be a treasure of information to A. V. Kidder. Like other pueblo people, the Pecos were active makers, users, and traders of pottery. Kidder identified eighteen different types of pottery that came into and went out of fashion at Pecos over the centuries. These changes in form and decoration, once the sequence was established, gave Kidder the clues he needed to trace the construction pattern of the pueblo. In the early days of the pueblo, the Pecos imported most of their decorated pottery from the Río Grande Valley. But about the time the pueblo reached its height (1500 to 1600), they began making a fine, polychrome ware of rich reds and browns with a thick, shiny glaze. Pottery from much of the Pueblo world found its way to Pecos—Zuni, Zia, Hopi, vessels from the Pajarito Plateau, as well as plains ware from the Texas Panhandle. After Spanish contact, some Pecos potters applied their skills to creating plates and candlesticks. More than 700 clay pipes and hundreds of human and animal effigies also were found in the trash mounds.

Throughout the ruins of the pueblo, Kidder found some 2,000 burials. Life span of the Pecos averaged around fifty years, although many of the remains were of young children under five years old. A majority of the burials were found in the trash—not a sign of disrespect but a matter of practicality. Possessing only stone and wood tools, the people found the soft trash mounds the easiest to dig. Individuals were buried with great care, usually with pottery and other possessions.

Two-thirds of the pueblo dwellings on the mesilla remain unexcavated. One day, far in the future, the silent ruins will reveal more of their secrets. But the valley still remains. One can look at the beauty and serenity of the place that was home for centuries and easily imagine the rich lives of the Pueblo people of Pecos.

PECOS — GATEWAY TO PUEBLOS & PLAINS

Glaze V Bowl, 1600–1700. The distinctive "awanyu," thought to be a feathered serpent,
was a popular design found on Pecos pottery for hundreds of years.

SIXTEENTH · CENTURY PECOS

was not only one of the largest and strongest of the pueblos, but was also a center for trade with nomadic plains buffalo hunters called "Teyas" and "Querechos," terms applied by the Pecos and Jemez Indians, then and now, to Apacheans.

These Apaches, already consummate plainsmen by Coronado's time, had arrived from the north around 1525, probably as the vanguard of a migration that left a loose but continuous chain of Apache bands in control of the High Plains from Canada into Texas. In New Mexico, thwarted in an attempt to take over some of the eastern pueblos, Apache invaders made peace with the inhabitants and returned to the plains. By 1540 an Apache-Pueblo trade had developed that was to evolve into close social and political alliances between the hunters and townsmen. This was especially true of Pecos, close to the plains and strategically located on the pass most readily negotiable by pedestrians and loaded pack animals. And at Pecos systematic archeology has revealed an influx of plains objects beginning in the second quarter of the sixteenth century.

Most of the year the Apaches lived among the buffalo they hunted, but at the onset of winter they sought the margins of the short-grass country. Besides those who Coronado's soldiers reported staying under the "wings" of Pecos, there were others who went to camp near the villages of Caddoan farmers in the tall-grass prairies: some to the Wichita country of central Kansas, known then as "Quivira," and others to settlements of Caddoan speakers to the southeast "toward Florida." Via the Apache network, news of these Caddoans got back to Pecos.

Various chroniclers of Coronado's expedition from Pecos to Quivira in 1541-1542 provide evidence that the Teyas and Querechos were uniquely adapted to life on the plains. Their well-tanned, thin-walled, sewn skin tents, carried by pack trains of dogs, enabled them not only to follow the herds and harvest enough meat and hides for themselves, but also to accumulate and transport a surplus of plains products to trade at settlements of horticultural peoples. Spanish observations indicate that these were the only Indians on the High Plains between

Quivira and the pueblos, not only in Coronado's time but for more than a century thereafter. Spanish colonists of circa 1600 found Indians with the same life style living in the same area, but called them "Vaqueros" ("cow herders") and "Vaquero Apaches." The name Apache was Aztec (Nahuatl) and probably originated among the numerous Nahuatl-speaking Mexican Indians accompanying Spanish expeditions. In Nahuatl "Apache" means "raccoon," a fact still known to native speakers of Spanish in New Mexico today.

In the 1600s both the bison herds and the volume of New Mexico trade with Plains Apaches continued to grow. In 1622 a Franciscan missionary stated that Apaches came by the hundreds from the plains to Pecos each year at harvest time to trade, and that some Apaches wintered "under the eaves" of the pueblo. Accounts of another Franciscan, published in the 1630s, indicated that the Vaquero Apaches were bringing, along with their families, pack trains of as many as five hundred dogs loaded with meat and hides into the Río Grande Valley, where Spanish colonists as well as Pueblo Indians had become dependent on the Apache trade. The colonists, with infrequent and inadequate supplies from Mexico, needed skins for clothing, and the Pueblo people, forced to pay "tribute" to the Spaniards, could satisfy them with buffalo hides. In the 1630s, after falling prey to Spanish slave raiders themselves, the Apaches tried to meet the Spanish need for slaves by adding another item of trade to their stock. They brought captured women and children, mainly Wichitas from Quivira, whom they usually traded for horses. Later, the Apaches brought in Caddoan slaves in such numbers that the good relations they had with some Caddoans came to an end. Ultimately (by 1686) Apache-Caddoan relations deteriorated all along the prairie borderlands.

In addition, dubious of Spanish good faith, Apache traders began to restrict their business to border pueblos, leading to the institution of the "trade fair" and increasing the importance of Pecos.

In 1675 Apaches called Faraones were declared the scourge of New Mexico, where they raided and harassed eastern Pueblo and Spanish settlement alike. However, some Faraones with close ties to Pecos maintained that friendship for the next half-century. After 1680, during the hiatus in Spanish rule that followed the Pueblo Rebellion, this intimacy increased and in the 1690s, at the time of the Spanish reconquest, Faraon Apaches were actually living with the people of Pecos. The Pecos people apparently valued their ties with the Apaches more than peace with the Spanish.

In 1711, at the annual fall trade fair, the Pecos Indians were said to have "always" been involved in trade with "Apache Indians, Faraones, Chipaynes, and Jacindes's" who came to their pueblo most years bringing buffalo meat, lard, grease, buckskins, buffalo hides or elk skins, and Indian captives. In turn, the Pecos sold these captives to the Spaniards as slaves at a profit. In the same period it was noted that the Pecos Indians, who were being paid in iron awls for church construction work in Santa Fe, were in turn trading these to Apaches for buffalo or elk skins or meat.

Although archeologic finds indicate contact

between the Indians of Pecos and the Jicarilla Apaches well before 1700, in that year some rebellious Pecos leaders escaped from prison in Santa Fe and took refuge in "La Jicarilla." After 1734 Pecos at times harbored the Mountain Band of the Jicarillas, the two groups making common cause against the Comanches. After 1750 Apaches called Palomas, Cuartelejos, and Carlanas took refuge in and near the pueblo after being forced off the central plains by Comanches and by Pawnees supplied with guns by the French.

In 1748 the parish priest of Taos reported Apaches called Jicarillas living near both Taos and Pecos pueblos. About 1752, also, 300 Carlana, Paloma, and Cuartelejo Apaches wintered near Pecos and left their women and children in the pueblo when they went to the plains to hunt buffalo. The next year, the Spanish Governor Tomás Vélez Cachupín reported that "A large portion of this [Apache] nation is present in the neighborhood of Pecos . . . except during the times when it is necessary for them to hunt buffalo or when some groups go back and forth to the plains to see their relatives."

Comanche hostility may well have been focused on Pecos because of its close ties with Apaches. After 1770, as a result of Comanche harassment, large-scale Apache trade at Pecos essentially terminated. In 1786 the Lipiyane Apaches, also called Llaneros by the Spaniards, came to Pecos and declared themselves part of the Jicarillas. As such, they requested Spanish permission to reestablish a commerce which they had carried on at Pecos Pueblo with settlers thirty-five or forty years before. These were the remnants of Carlanas, Palomas, and Cuartelejos who had frequented the pueblo around 1750. But they had meanwhile committed depredations elsewhere in Texas and in northern Mexico and were therefore denied entrance. They were able to infiltrate New Mexico, however, where they eventually became known as the Jicarillas' Llanero or Plains Band. In 1791 a party of Llanero and Mescalero Apaches did come to Pecos to trade, but by then commerce and alliance with Comanches had become much more important to Spaniards and Pecos Indians alike, and occasional deaths of Pecos Indians were attributed to Apaches. In 1838, the pueblo was abandoned after three centuries of action-packed history on the New Mexico frontier.

As mentioned earlier, Apache presence at Pecos is reflected in the pueblo's stratified trash heaps by an influx of Plains-style stone artifacts, primarily of Alibates flint from the Texas Panhandle. The first appearance of these items in the mid-1500s marks, beyond reasonable doubt, the advent of the Teyas and Querechos, or Apaches, who controlled that area and monopolized the Plains-Pecos trade. Also, a tipi-ring site on the Pecos River near Anton Chico has yielded Pecos glaze sherds that could date from Coronado's time; it may have been a way-station for Apaches traveling between the Texas Panhandle and Pecos. Another tipi-ring site, northeast of Las Vegas, New Mexico, apparently served a similar function in the mid-1600s. And on the other side of the Plains, Pecos Pueblo potsherds found in Wichita sites in central Kansas, and made in the 1500s, 1600s and early 1700s may well have been carried there by Apache traders.

APACHES AT PECOS

Some of the distinctive stone artifacts found at Pecos, but restricted elsewhere to the Dismal River (Plains Apache) complex in western Kansas and Nebraska, were probably left at Pecos by those Apache visitors who later (circa 1800) became the Llanero Band of the modern Jicarillas. Moreover, tubular pottery pipes of the style made at Pecos have been recovered from Dismal River sites, further documenting Pecos-Plains Apache interaction. And sherds of pottery from Pecos spanning a period from 1600 to 1750 have been found at various Apache sites in northeastern New Mexico.

There is other archeological evidence of Apaches at Pecos. In the area apparently most favored by Apache visitors, immediately east of the church, was excavated the remains of a simple, adobe-covered pole structure that had burned while still occupied. Among other artifacts found on the floor were four crushed pottery vessels, two Pueblo and two Jicarilla, and a worked fragment of a Chinese porcelain cup made in the mid-1600s. More common in the near vicinity of Pecos than early Jicarilla pottery (called Ocate Micaceous), is a type attributed to the Faraon Apaches. Called Perdido Plain, this ware has been found as far east as Sayre, Oklahoma.

The story of Apache-Pecos relations, culled from documents and punctuated with archeological artifacts, is one of the most interesting chapters in the history of the Pueblo Southwest.

PECOS
―――――――
1540 · 1846

VI CICUYE & THE FIRST SPANIARDS
JOSEPH P. SANCHEZ

IT WAS AUTUMN in the upper Pecos Valley, 1540. The serrated mountains dazzled with a giant quilt of fall colors under a pale blue sky. In the foothills, the arroyos left little trace of the summer rains that had scoured ravine and gully alike. Above the sweeping curve of one arroyo, the fortress-pueblo of Cicuye (later known as Pecos) crowned a high bluff of piñon and chamisa. Below, under the village walls in fields that had begun to turn brown, a mild sun warmed men, women, and children gathering maize. Warriors stood guard over the pueblo. In the distance a small column of helmeted Spanish soldiers, led by Indian guides, pulled their tired horses across the brushy high country of the mesa world to Cicuye. Among them walked a brown-robed Franciscan friar, tattered and sweaty, with a single vision of spiritual conquest in his mind.

As Captain Hernando de Alvarado and his men, the advance guard of the Coronado Expedition, wended their way through the mountain pass to the pueblo, they realized that they were the first Europeans to walk that land. Not quite fifty years had passed since Christopher Columbus had claimed the Caribbean for his Catholic Majesties. In that short time Spanish mariners looking for legendary civilizations and a mysterious strait across the continent had run the Atlantic coast from Labrador to the Strait of Magellan. As the Age of Discovery unfolded, explorers crossed the Americas to the Pacific Ocean, Hernán Cortes swiftly conquered Tenochtitlán, heart of the Aztec dominion, and the Pizarro brothers struggled to overrun the last Inca stronghold. As the period neared its end, explorers believed they could discover "another Mexico" or "another Peru," but the fabled Seven Cities of Antillia, the Fountain of Youth, El Dorado and Gran Quivira lay always beyond their reach, *mas allá*.

Cartographers like Abraham Ortelius mapped the course of each Spanish explorer across the New World with the studied eye of a scholar-monk. Greek and Roman mythological figures, sea monsters, and ornate compass roses illuminated their maps and enhanced the mysterious place names of the real and imagined geography they recorded. The mapmakers sat by the hour and marveled at the strange stories behind each name. And now, one lifetime after Columbus's landing, Alvarado stood outside the walls of yet another place,

CICUYE & THE FIRST SPANIARDS

Cicuye, on the edge of a vast plain that stretched to mid-continent of North America. Cicuye was expecting them.

Whence came the Spaniards? Through traders and slaves, the pueblos had received vague and varied word of events along the Gulf Coast, Mexico and the Sonoran wastelands. Long before they beheld Alvarado's bearded visage and heard the snort and neigh of a Spanish horse, the pueblos knew of the white man and his terrible weapons. Then there was the story of four men, one of them black, who had traversed the continent and crossed the southern end of the "Río Grande" which ran through the Pueblo world. The Spaniards knew well the details of Cabeza de Vaca, Estevan the Moor and two other companions, who, lost for eight years, crossed the wilds of North America from Texas to Sonora where they were finally rescued. The black man later returned to search for the Seven Cities, but instead he met his death at the hands of the Zuni at Hawikuh. When a large Spanish army led by Francisco Vásquez de Coronado appeared outside of Hawikuh, the Zunis thought he had come to avenge the black man. He hadn't. After the Zuni provoked a battle, the Spaniards attacked and defeated them. Coronado held Hawikuh through the summer and discussed peace with Zuni leaders.

Word of the battle spread quickly among the pueblos. Thirteen days distant from Hawikuh, the headmen of Cicuye held council. Impressed by Spanish arms and might, they decided to send a peace delegation to Coronado. When they arrived, the general received them cordially. The Spaniards quickly dubbed their spokesman "Bigotes," because he wore a long mustache. Bigotes offered Coronado gifts of native shields, feathered headdresses, and some curious large hides of tangled and wooly hair, brown in color and coarse to the touch. Months later, on the plains, the Spaniards would see the "monstrous cows," the source of the heavy hides. Coronado reciprocated with an assortment of artificial pearls, glassware, and jingle bells.

Determined to receive formal homage from Cicuye and to learn more about the cattle with the coarse hair, Coronado assigned Captain Alvarado to return with the Bigotes delegation to their land. By early October, the first Europeans entered Cicuye.

Like Acoma set so high on a rock "that it would require a good musket to land a ball on top," Cicuye too impressed the Spaniards. Chronicler Pedro de Castañeda described Cicuye as:

> . . . a pueblo containing about 500 warriors. It is feared throughout the land. It is square, perched on a rock in the center of a vast patio or plaza with its estufas. The houses are all alike, four stories high. One can walk on the roofs over the whole pueblo, there being no streets to prevent this. The second terrace is all surrounded with lanes which enable one to circle the whole pueblo. The lanes are like balconies which project out and under which one may find shelter. The houses have no doors on the ground floor. The inhabitants use movable ladders to climb the corridors which are on the inner side of the pueblos. They enter them that way, as the doors of the houses open into the corridors on this terrace. The corridors are used as streets. The houses facing the open country are

back to back with those on the patio and in time of war they are entered through the interior ones. The pueblo is surrounded by a low stone wall. Inside there is a water spring, which can be diverted from them. The people of this town pride themselves because no one has been able to subjugate them, while they dominate the pueblos they wish.

Before his sojourn to Cicuye had ended, Alvarado had met the two objectives Coronado required of him. First, he exacted from his hosts a sort of acknowledgment of Spanish sovereignty over the pueblo. Second, he had with Indian guides gone out to the plains and seen the shaggy cattle. But more important, he had learned that Quivira lay to the east of Cicuye, somewhere beyond the buffalo plains he had discovered for Spain.

"Acochis," said El Turco, the Indian guide who looked like a Turk to the soldiers. Sitting around their campfire on the plains, the Spaniards asked him again. He repeated the word "acochis," and the Spaniards thought he meant "gold." Quivira rich in gold lay somewhere toward the rising sun, and El Turco promised to lead them there. He told them so many stories of riches that the Spaniards did not care to see any more cattle, and as soon as they had spotted a few herds they turned back to report the news to their general. El Turco went with them.

Back on the Rio Grande in the province of Tiguex, Alvarado, his men, and El Turco joined other Spaniards who had set up winter camp at one of the pueblos in advance of the general and his army. When Coronado arrived, Alvarado told him of his visit to Cicuye and the plains. Somewhere to the east beyond Cicuye, said Alvarado, was Quivira. First, Coronado was eager to see Cicuye.

Meanwhile, El Turco brewed trouble between the Spaniards and Cicuye. He told Coronado that he had a golden bracelet which Bigotes had taken. The general sent his captain to Cicuye to get it. At Cicuye the people received Alvarado in friendship. Anxiously, he awaited Bigotes's reply through translators.
El Cacique, an elderly headman,

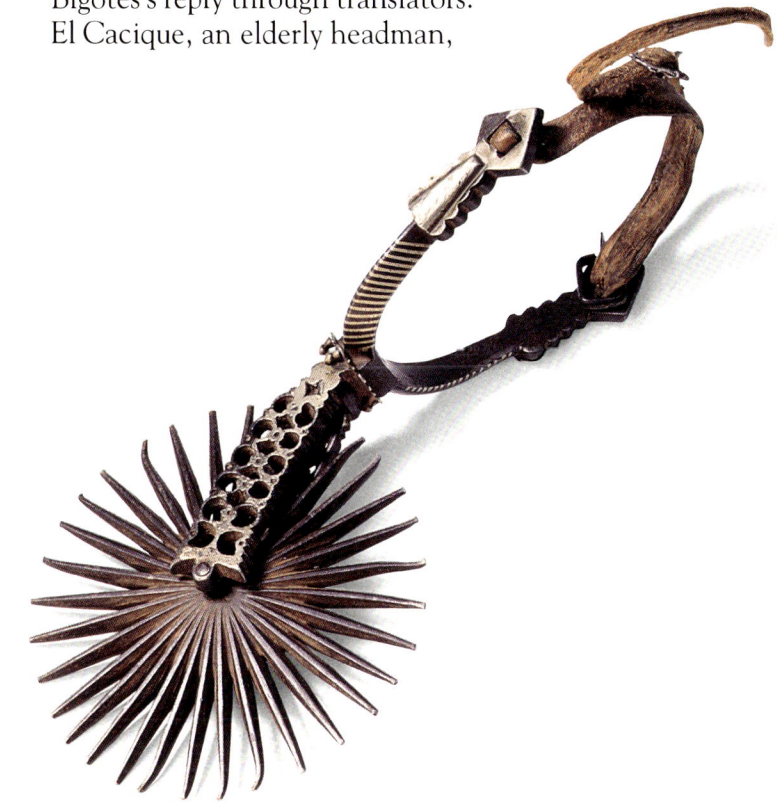

Seventeenth century Spanish spur (espuela). One of many "new" metal items that must have astounded the Indians.

CICUYE & THE FIRST SPANIARDS

stood by him saying that El Turco lied about the bracelet. When the Spaniard saw no other recourse, he persuaded Bigotes and El Cacique to come to his tent. Upon their arrival the Spaniards seized them and put them in chains. They were kept prisoners for Tiguex. "This," wrote Castañeda, "was the beginning of the distrust the Indians had from then on." The friendship was broken. El Turco, once a captive of Cicuye, surely smiled with glee.

At Tiguex the Indians were disturbed by the imprisonment of Bigotes and Cacique in their pueblo. Ill feeling spread against Coronado and his men. Spanish improprieties outraged the people of Tiguex who declared war against the invaders. But European weapons and horses were too much for them; and after weeks of resistance they were defeated, unmercifully some thought.

During the Tiguex War, Coronado decided to go to Cicuye. He took the elderly Cacique and set him free, promising that when he went to Quivira he would free Bigotes and leave him with his people. Amidst great rejoicing at seeing Cacique free, the people of Cicuye received Coronado in peace. After visiting the pueblo and talking to the Indians, the general returned to his army at Tiguex.

By early spring 1541, the army had departed Tiguex for the plains in search of Quivira. They stopped at Cicuye and released Bigotes. The inhabitants were friendly and furnished provisions. Later Castañeda wrote: "Bigotes and the Cacique gave the general a young boy named Xabe, a native of Quivira, so that he might get information from him about the land. This boy said that there was gold and silver there but not in the quantities stated by the Turk."

On the way El Turco went along as a guide. Traveling southeasterly toward the plains, they followed the mountain range and river east of Cicuye. After four days they turned eastward to the river which flowed from the north. Coronado named it Río de Cicuye. The army stopped to build a bridge across it; four days later, the entire army and livestock walked over the bridge on their way to Quivira. From there they marched toward the rising sun onto the plains of the Texas Panhandle.

After ten days the Spaniards met a nomadic people called Querechos. These people hunted the buffalo on foot as they had not yet acquired the horse which they now saw for the first time. As nomads, they lived in tents made from buffalo skins. When they saw the Spaniards "they did not move away or disturb themselves in the least," wrote Castañeda. They were unafraid.

El Turco came to the fore and spoke to them. It seemed they spoke of Quivira. The Querechos pointed in the direction of the rising sun and told them of a long river that they could follow for ninety days, going from one settlement to another. El Turco embellished their report. But after long, warm days of wandering through the treeless plains, doubts of the Turk's truthfulness arose among the Spaniards. In the expedition was a tattooed Indian, a native of Quivira named Ysopete. He persisted in saying that the Turk lied. Slowly the Spaniards began to believe him instead. Somewhere on the plains near present-day Oklahoma, the army held council.

Coronado declared that they had been deceived by El Turco. They agreed to split the army: thirty-six men and the general would continue toward Quivira, and the rest of the army would return to Tiguex.

With El Turco in chains, the general followed his guides; among them was Ysopete. Forty-eight days later they reached Quivira. Obviously Quivira was not the great kingdom of untold wealth they had sought. When asked why he had guided them so perversely, El Turco confessed that

> the people of Cicuye had asked him to take the Spaniards out there and lead them astray on the plains. Thus, through lack of provisions, their horses would die and they themselves would become so feeble that, upon their return, the people of Cicuye would kill them easily, and so obtain revenge for what the Spaniards had done to them.

Ysopete, his nemesis, looked on. Then the Spaniards grabbed El Turco and garroted him. Coronado turned his detachment of soldiers around and his Indian guides headed west toward the setting sun.

Meanwhile, the main army had returned to Tiguex by way of Cicuye, which they found to be unfriendly. At Tiguex the army settled to await the return of Coronado. As the general was overdue by mid-August and there was talk that he would be ambushed at Cicuye, Tristan de Luna y Arrellano left Tiguex with forty men. When Don Tristan arrived at Cicuye, the people came out to fight. "This caused the Spaniards to tarry four days to inflict some punishment on them, as was done, because a few shots fired into the pueblo killed some of their people." They would not come out into the open because "on the first day, two of their prominent men were killed," reported Castañeda. If the people of Cicuye hoped to destroy the Spanish command easily, they had much to learn about Spanish determination.

It took Coronado more than a month to return with his half-starved troops. After his return, he must have reflected on the day he left Tiguex and that El Turco had asked him why had they loaded their horses with so many provisions. The wiley Indian had reasoned that the horses would tire and not be able to carry back all the gold and silver they would find. In retrospect, Coronado could clearly see the deceit which had been played upon him by El Turco and the people of Cicuye.

Although Coronado departed Cicuye in peace, he was not inclined to return there or to the plains. Father Juan de Padilla and Fray Luis de Úbeda hoped to persuade him otherwise but to no avail. Padilla and a small escort eventually departed Cicuye to create a mission field in the plains. Fray Luis was last seen by Spaniards who observed the Indians leading him away from their pueblo. They had foresaken the Christian God and all things Spanish.

A year and a half had passed since Alvarado and his men first stood out side the gates of Cicuye. Much had happened between the two people in that time. And now the pueblo world watched from a distance as Coronado's army moved west beyond the big river whence they came. Neither Cicuye nor the other pueblos could know how much their lives would be changed by his visitation.

VII GASPAR CASTAÑO DE SOSA & CICUYE
JOSEPH P. SANCHEZ

On a cold, snowy December morning in 1590, sentries of Cicuye alerted the pueblo to a small group of helmeted Spanish horse soldiers who stood outside their walls. Through signs, the warriors learned that the ten or so thin-looking bearded Spaniards asked only for food. They gave them maize. The exhausted Spaniards spent the day at the pueblo, and the Indians lodged them in the plaza for the night. The next day the soldiers went among the people unarmed so as not to alarm them and asked for more food. Suddenly there was a great outcry, and at the same time many stones and arrows were shot at them. Quickly the Spaniards scurried about for their weapons, but some of the warriors had come down from the roof tops and carried off most of their arms. The Spaniards grabbed what they could to defend themselves and dashed to their horses. Riding bareback they fled the pueblo. Afterwards the Indians divided the booty for their own use. In the attack the Spaniards lost five harquebuses, eleven swords, nineteen saddles, nine sets of armor and some wearing apparel and bed clothes. Knowing the Spaniards would return, the people of Cicuye prepared to defend themselves against a larger force. For now they could only wonder, whence came the Spaniards?

For nearly forty years after Coronado's initial visit, the north country was all but ignored except for a few traders, prospectors, or slavers who may have crossed the Río Grande into New Mexico. Between 1581 and 1583, two small expeditions, one led by Francisco Chamuscado Sánchez and a subsequent one led by Antonio de Espejo, had visited the Pueblo world and had seen Coronado's Cicuye. Indeed, Espejo's men claimed that they had even attacked a large pueblo with a similar sounding name, but with little result. Their reports of New Mexico as a land with potential mineral wealth, nevertheless, interested speculators who hoped to gain concessions from the crown to monopolize it. And Franciscan friars prayed that they could soon return and convert the Puebloans to Christianity. By the 1590s, Spanish officials in Mexico City had, once again, begun to turn their attention to the north.

Meanwhile, the Spanish crown had pondered the pacification of the north country. As bidders for the contract played a political game to influence their chances in the competition, an unexpected situation unfolded in Nuevo León on New Spain's northeastern

frontier south of the Río Grande. Gaspar Castaño de Sosa, lieutenant governor of Nuevo León, had inherited the leadership of the province when governor Luis de Carvajal had been jailed by the Inquisition on charges of being a crypto-Jew. Although Castaño carried out his obligations dutifully, he had a plan of his own. Based on privileges implicit in the king's concessions to Carvajal, Don Gaspar decided to colonize New Mexico himself. Spanish officials held his actions were illegal, but nonetheless the lieutenant governor persisted in what he believed to be right and just.

Castaño's argument soon took on a history of its own. Before long Viceroy Marques de Villamanrique had developed a file on the case. When Castaño sent agents to Mexico City to argue in his favor, the viceroy paid them no mind. In 1590, the viceroy warned his successor that Castaño and his followers were "outlaws, criminals and murderers—who practice neither justice nor piety and are raising a rebellion in defiance of God and King. These men invade the interior, seize peaceable Indians, and sell them in Mazapil, Saltillo, Sombrerete, and everywhere in the region."

The new viceroy, Don Luis de Velasco II, took heed. He sent Captain Juan Morlete with a message for Castaño to cease his slaving activities and cancel his plans to go to New Mexico. On a warm June day in 1590 the two men met in the dusty mining town of Nueva Almadén. Castaño took Morlete's warning with a grain of salt. As quickly as he had arrived, Morlete departed. The two men, however, would meet again twenty months hence and Morlete would hold the upper hand.

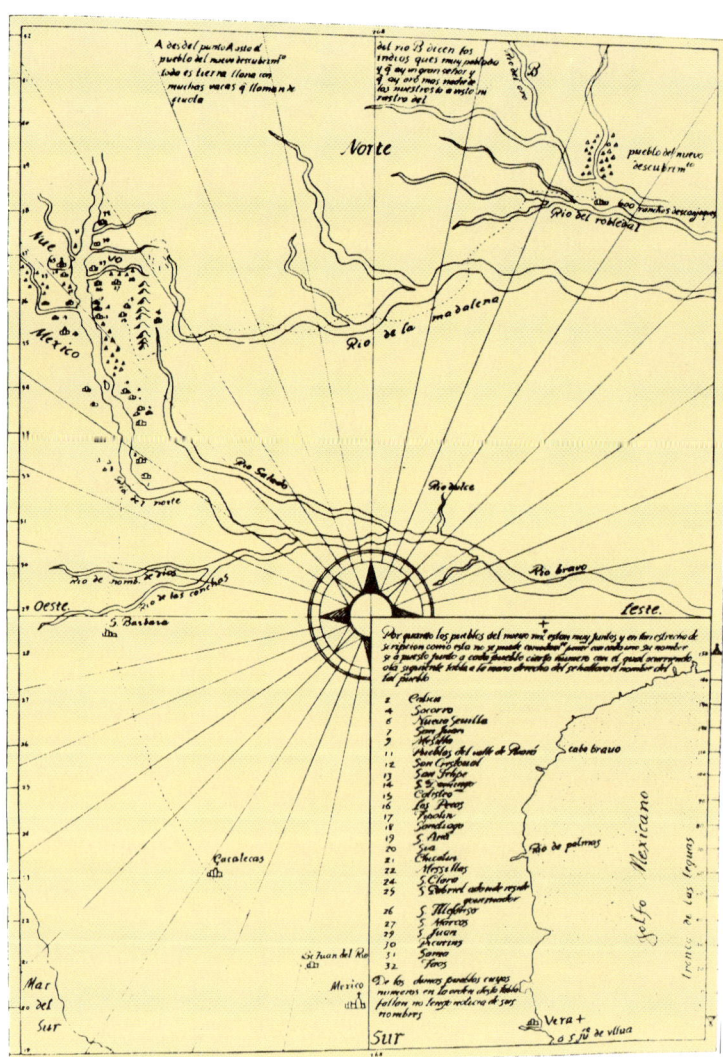

Map of New Mexico, c. 1602, by Enrique Martinez. The Pueblo de los Pecos is no. 16.

Unmoved by the warning, the charismatic Castaño addressed the people of Nueva Almadén about his well-known intentions to settle New Mexico. Don Gaspar reasoned that a grateful king would reward their efforts to expand the area of pacification and settlements at no cost to the crown. Convinced their leader was right, nearly 200 men, women, and children packed their belongings on carts and prepared to follow him.

On Friday, 27 July 1590, the slow-moving, creaky, oxen-pulled carreta caravan pulled out of Nueva Almadén. Six weeks later they reached the Río Grande near present day Ciudad Acuña. After more weeks of traversing the dry and barren land, their scouts led them to the waters of the Pecos River, which because of its brackishness, they called "el Río Salado." Throughout the fall months the lumbering caravan followed the Pecos and by early December passed the sandy hill country near today's Carlsbad, New Mexico.

At one of their camps on the plains of southeastern New Mexico, Castaño called his men together. He figured that they were not far from one of the first pueblos. In anticipation of making contact, Don Gaspar instructed his men not to enter any Indian town. Scouts would be sent to gather information, and if they could capture one or two Indian informants they should learn the strengths and weaknesses of the pueblo. But the first pueblo was still far away from them.

The first scouting party went out on December 2. Led by Maese de Campo Cristóbal de Heredia, the eleven-man detachment returned twice in two weeks for food and to report that no pueblo had been seen. They went out again and on December 13, one of the men returned to report that the advance group was following an Indian trail. A week passed with no word from the scouting party. Castaño became concerned lest some disaster had befallen his men. On December 23, a cold wind swept the plains as Don Gaspar and Andrés Pérez, the administrative secretary, stood on a hill and, in the distance, they observed a man "on foot with his harquebus across his shoulders and a horse in front, tired without a saddle." It was Juan Rodríguez Nieto, one of their scouts. Bruised, cold, hungry, and fatigued, he told them of the surprise attack they had suffered at a pueblo they would later identify as Cicuye. Somehow the men had survived three days and two nights in freezing temperatures. They had been saved from starvation by an Indian woman they had met along the way, who had given them each a handful of cornmeal to eat. Luckily, warriors from the pueblo did not pursue them. Before long the rest of the battered soldiers, with three wounded men, arrived to tell their story of woe. Undaunted, Castaño de Sosa determined to go soon to the large pueblo and recover their property before the Indians could destroy it.

Castaño spent Christmas Day selecting and outfitting twenty men, some of whom had been to the pueblo. The next day they departed with seventeen servants, and, four days later they were in sight of the pueblo. As night fell they camped and prepared for the next day.

Before dawn on December 31 the soldiers were up and slowly saddled their horses in the cold winter air, while some of their servants prepared breakfast and others packed up the camp. Standing by the campfires to warm themselves, the men ate quietly. As Castaño spoke, he paused periodically to gather his thoughts about how to approach the Indians without provoking them. Their whole desire and intent was, he said, "to do them no harm at all." After the plan had been explained and the orders given, they set out for the pueblo.

Martín de Salazar and Diego de Biruega ran ahead of the detachment which marched slowly with banners flying high. The two men approached the Indians and tried to communicate that they had come in peace. But they were unable to convince the warriors of their purpose. When Castaño and the main body came near the pueblo, he ordered that the trumpets be blown.

Riding at a gallop, his scouts returned and reported that the whole pueblo was armed, "men and women on the roof tops and down below, with great preparation." Don Gaspar ordered a camp established at "an harquebus shot from the pueblo, on the side where it seemed to be the strongest." Two bronze cannon were placed and readied for firing. He ordered all should be prepared in case of "some effrontery like the previous one" against the advance party the previous week.

When all was arranged, Castaño called to the Indians. None was willing to leave the security of the pueblo to parley with him. It appeared to be a standoff. It was eight o'clock in the morning, the beginning of one of the longest days in Cicuye's history.

Pecos appeared formidable; the Spaniards could see its defenses. Ramparts had been constructed to complement the defensive walls and narrow passages which were staggered in a way that the attackers could not easily gain a long passageway to enter the pueblo. The people were armed with slings and stones, as well as bows, arrows, and clubs. Later, the Spaniards learned that the pueblo had been at war with other tribes, and the fortifications had been up for some time.

Castaño hoped to avoid an assault against the heavily protected walls of Pecos. He wondered what thirty-eight men could do against the Indian pueblo. With five men, Castaño again approached Pecos to try to convince the Indians to "understand that we did not come to harm them." Instead they jeered him as their women hastily carried stones up to the roof tops "because the men were all armed at their posts and giving loud cries in high spirits." By now Don Gaspar and the others rode their horses around the whole pueblo holding up ornaments, giving signs of peace, and shouting words of friendship. Several times in five hours six horsemen rode around Cicuye while the Indians slung rocks and shot arrows at them. All the while the din from the pueblo grew louder as the Indians taunted and jeered them from behind the walls and roof tops of their fortified pueblo. After noon, Castaño returned to his main camp, took some knives and other trifles and again approached the pueblo. This time the Indians took the gifts he offered and he was able to speak to "the captain of the pueblo." Despite the gifts, Castaño failed to make friends with the people of Cicuye.

Back at camp Don Gaspar called a council to discuss the perplexing situation. "Señores compañeros," he said,

Glaze III olla. A distinctive Pecos style of the 1500s.

"what do your honors think? These Indians do not want our friendship." He explained he wanted to pacify them; and if possible with no harm done to one side or the other. One of the soldiers replied, "Your grace should not waste time on that because it is useless." The mood of the men had changed, they would pacify the pueblo rather than leave an enemy to their backs when they moved on to the Río Grande. But Castaño hoped to give Cicuye one more chance. He called Andrés Pérez to go with him to the pueblo as a witness. Again they rode their horses around the village as the Indians demonstrated against him. After a while the Spaniards returned to camp.

Castaño resumed the war council. "What shall we do, Señores, since these Indians do not want to be docile?" he asked. "Why does your grace wait for these dogs?" replied one of the angry soldiers. Again, Don Gaspar inquired, "Well then, what do your honors desire that we do?" They responded that the Indians should be chastised severely "since they could not make good friends of them." Wavering in his resolve to punish Cicuye, he responded, "It seems to me, Señores Compañeros, that it is already too late for us to conduct this affair as your honors say." The little camp of Spaniards appeared powerless against the large fortified pueblo in the background. Yet Castaño's men persisted in their ambitious plan to capture the place. After some discussion they presented their leader with the mandate, "If the victory is God's to give us, we have time and more to spare." There was time in the day for an attack. In discussing the battle plan, Castaño ordered his men not to shoot to kill. He hoped only to intimidate his enemy.

The Indians watched the sun between the clouds as it began its descent toward the western sky. The Spaniards reckoned it was after two o'clock when they took their positions for the assault on Cicuye. From their roof tops the warriors could see two Spaniards move around their north side to an elevation behind the pueblo. Then they saw the Spanish leader ride up to one of the walls and shout something to them. When one of their women threw some ashes at him, the Indians gave a loud shout. On the west side of the pueblo, warriors counterattacked five armored men who attempted to climb the wall of an isolated building. The Spaniards reached the roof top anyway. One of them pulled up a small artillery piece, moved it into position, loaded it and fired it. In an effort to intimidate the warriors, his companions fired their harquebuses. But the Indians hurled more stones at them and shot a volley of arrows to the roof top. In the midst of the fight, they saw the Spanish leader ride up to the pueblo again. He called out to them; they did not understand him. Besides, it was too late, their pueblo was under attack.

Castaño withdrew and rallied his men to attack the strongest force of Indians to dislodge them. But the warriors held their posts. Suddenly, the warriors who had fought so valiantly, lost their resolve. The Spaniards quickly noticed it and took advantage of the situation. Later, they described the moment when

> an Indian servant of the said Lieutenant [Castaño], named Tomás, being very near to this houseblock, began to shoot at them with bows and arrows and another Indian, named Miguel, did the same.

When the Indians [of the pueblo] saw that ours were shooting at them, they took fright and showed more fear than at [the fire of] the harquebuses. So the Lieutenant commanded that we should press them from all sides, and this was done.

Tomás and Domingo Hernández, two Portuguese, were among the first to enter a house. Before long the Indians began to withdraw. The pueblo was now enveloped. On the south side where Castaño had camped, seventeen armed men without armor positioned a cannon on the pueblo. Two men on the mesa to the north watched to give warning if any Indians tried to escape from the pueblo. A small force aggressively prevented any movement on the west side. And Castaño with the main force attacked the east walls of the pueblo and gained a position on the roof of one block of houses. The Indians withdrew into their rooms as the Spaniards cleared the passageways leading to the central plaza. During this stage of the battle the fighting intensified. To make the Indians surrender and lessen his casualties, Castaño ordered his men to fire at will. Once the Plaza was gained, the firing stopped.

Don Gaspar surveyed the quieted pueblo that moments before was filled with the sounds of battle. He walked about the plaza, the Indians watched him from their houses. Not a shot was fired or stone thrown. Slowly some Indians emerged from hiding. Making the sign of the cross with their hands and saying "amigo, amigo, amigo," they signaled surrender. Some fled from the pueblo, while others refused to come out. Castaño again tried to explain that he did not come to make war on them. He requested the armor, saddles, harquebuses, swords, and clothing that had been taken from his advance guard the week before. One of the warriors explained that all of the saddles had been burned and the clothing had been distributed to other pueblos. All that remained of the swords was the blades. As night fell, Castaño ordered that the rest of the Spanish property should be brought to him the next day.

Castaño's Spaniards and the people of Cicuye began the European New Year with an uneasy peace. Don Gaspar had no plans to remain there. Once the rest of his wagon train had arrived, they rested a while, and on January 6 they moved on to the Río Grande pueblos. Months later, Castaño and his settlers were ousted from the pueblo world, not by Indians but by order of the viceroy, who had learned that Castaño and his people were illegally in New Mexico. Juan Morlete, the viceroy's representative, rode into the pueblo of Santo Domingo and arrested Castaño for trespassing into New Mexico without official license. Once Morlete had escorted the Castaño party from the land, the pueblos were once again freed of the Spaniards. But their respite would be temporary.

As for Castaño, he was tried, convicted, and in 1595 sentenced by order of the king of Spain to six years of exile from New Spain and assigned to service in the Philippine galleons. Should he default in his service, he would be liable to the death penalty. But Castaño's luck had run out; he died in a Chinese uprising against Spanish authority in the islands. Later, his name was cleared of the alleged crimes which had led to his conviction. Meanwhile, Spanish officials had not given up on pacifying New Mexico and opening it for settlement. On October 4, 1593, Viceroy Luis de Velasco informed the king that "preparations and negotiations" were underway for the settlement of New Mexico. It would be, however, five years before the next wagon train would roll its creaky wheels toward the north country.

VIII PECOS MISSION IN THE SEVENTEENTH CENTURY
JOSEPH P. SANCHEZ

From the time that Fray Luis de Úbeda first conceived the missionary potential of Cicuye in 1541, to the day that Fray Fernando de Velasco, guardian of the convento at Pecos, died at the hands of Indian rebels in the Pueblo Revolt of 1680, the padres had influenced Pecos Pueblo unalterably. Although the Indians resisted the change, the Franciscan friars persisted in their ministry until a coexistence, at least, had been achieved. Úbeda, however, had learned what his brethren would later know. The long history of conversion at Pecos would be fraught with toleration and resistance, and finally rebellion and respite as the two cultures jousted, one for survival, the other for dominance.

Rather than face the long walk back to New Spain with the Coronado expedition, the aged Fray Luis de Úbeda chose to spend his last days among the people of Cicuye. As Francisco Vásquez de Coronado turned his army away from New Mexico in April 1542, he sent Fray Luis provisions and a flock of sheep. The soldiers who herded the sheep to Cicuye were the last Europeans to see him alive. Of the event the chronicler Pedro de Castañeda wrote:

> Before the army set out from Tiguex, the men who were taking him a certain number of sheep he had coming met him accompanied by people on the way to visit other pueblos which were fifteen or twenty leagues from Cicuye. This gave rise to no little hope that he was in the good graces of the pueblo and that his instruction would bear fruit, even though he complained that the old men were forsaking him and he believed that in the end they would kill him.

Later, in the middle seventeenth century, Fray Antonio Tello, the Franciscan chronicler, reported an account of dubious origin that the Indians had assured the Spaniards that the old friar would be treated kindly. After Coronado's soldiers last saw him, it was believed that Fray Luis had returned to Cicuye where he had been given lodging. Each morning, as the story went, the Indians brought him "atole and tortillas" without speaking to him. To them the Christian priest would say "May God convert you!" Tello's story, however exaggerated as it may appear, gives a moral and heroic character to Úbeda in his last days. But the Cicuye of 1542 felt only bitterness toward the Spaniards who had

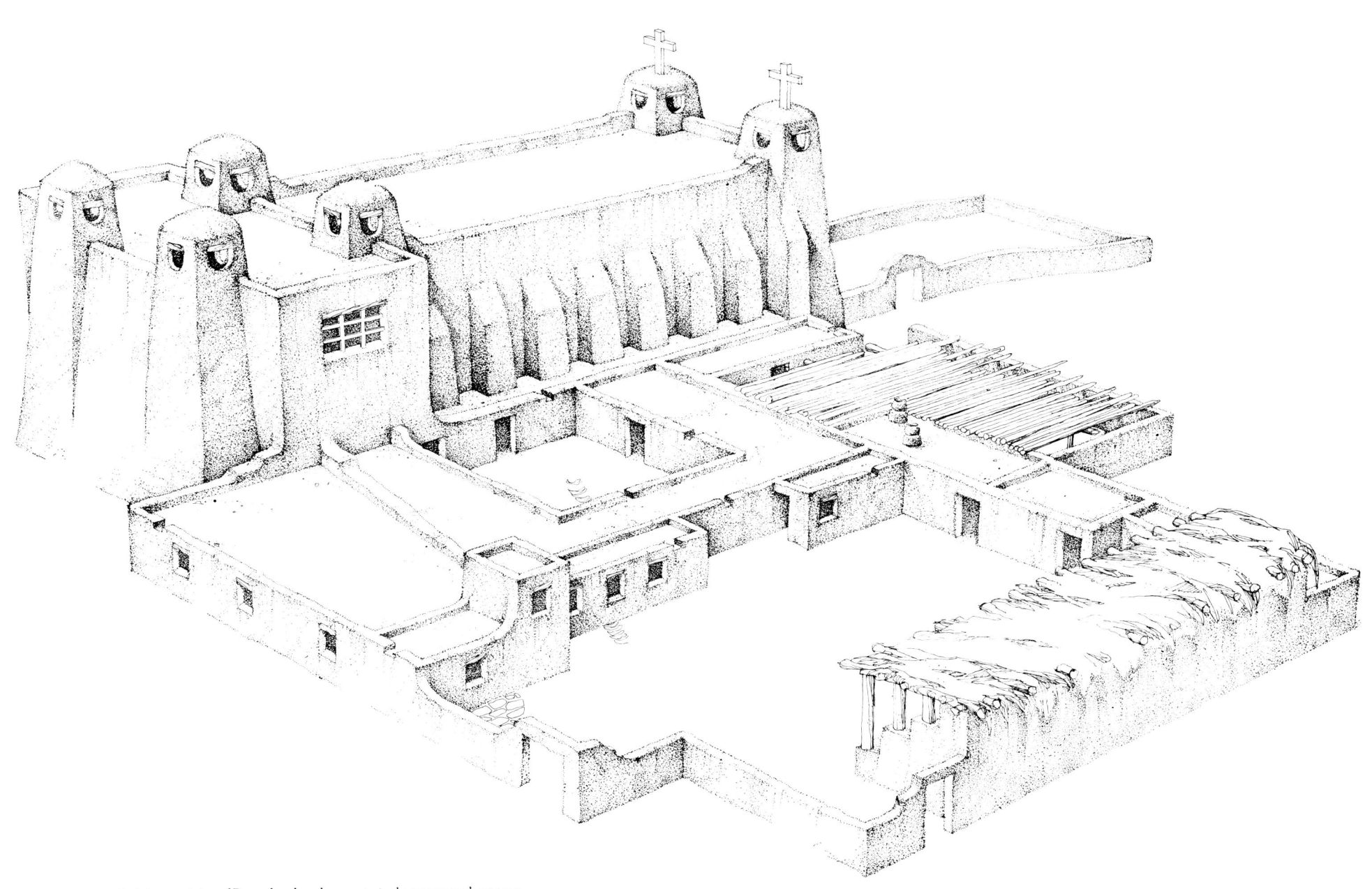
Artist's conception of Pecos church and convento in the seventeenth century.

come in peace but made war against its people, captured its leaders, and killed some of its warriors. There was little reason to expect the Pecoseños to accept the old padre and his Christian teachings. Still, Brother Luis with a "chisel and adze" hoped to erect a wooden cross at Cicuye and baptize "the children he found on the verge of death and send them to heaven." It would at least be a beginning.

For fifty-eight years after Coronado, Spanish contact with Pecos was all but forgotten except for the vaguely described visit there by Francisco Sánchez Chamuscado and his men in 1581, Antonio de Espejo's intimidation of "Ciquique" in 1582, and Gaspar Castaño de Sosa's attack on the fortress pueblo in 1590. During those decades the Franciscans at Santa Barbara, Chihuahua, dreamed of the north country and its pueblos, ripe for Christianity. In 1598, after years of promoting the potential New Mexican mission field, they returned, this time with Juan de Oñate, who had a royal contract to settle the Province of New Mexico. With Oñate and his settlers, Fray Alonso Martínez and nine Franciscans made the arduous trip northward to the pueblo world.

Wending its way from Santa Barbara to *"el paso del norte"* thence up the Río Grande, Oñate's wagon train had traveled for months before it reached the site of San Juan de los Caballeros in northern New Mexico. As soon as the Spaniards established themselves in their camps, Oñate visited the pueblos, exacted an oath of loyalty from those present, and assigned missionaries to work among them. On June 25, 1598, Don Juan and sixty

Bulto, St. Francis of Assisi. The Pecos mission was named after the town in Italy—Portiúncula—where St. Francis started the Franciscan order.

62

horsemen rode out to Pecos to receive "homage and obedience" from its inhabitants. Wisely, the Pecos chose not to fight the Spaniards, but instead listened patiently.

By mid-September the Pecos knew that their priest was named Fray Francisco de San Miguel. He was an elderly man, and like many Franciscans, Fray Francisco was accustomed to the rigors of frontier life. His assignment not only included Pecos but the vast area that stretched from Pecos to the Sandia Mountains and southward to the nearby "pueblos of the salines" along the Manzano Mountains. Little is known about his work among the Pecos, who doubtless tolerated the slowly progressing ministry.

Some structures, one of them a small church, had been constructed by the early 1620s. Although the earliest known structure probably dated to 1617, Fray Alonso de Benavides, Franciscan *custos* of the New Mexico missions, credited Fray Andrés Suárez with building, in 1622, the convento and a "church of peculiar construction and beauty . . . with room for all the people of the pueblo." The church was dedicated to Nuestra Señora de los Ángeles de Porciúncula. Later, eighteenth-century Franciscan chronicler, Agustín de Vetancourt, heard it described as "a magnificent temple adorned with six towers, three on each side." By mid-seventeenth century the mission at Pecos served "1189 souls" and its church, probably the largest European structure north of the Santa Barbara-Parral frontier, had been constructed on the south end of the pueblo's narrow mesa. Its facade faced east.

The Pecos mission, with church and convento, was nothing more than a program for the conversion of the Pecos to Christianity. As a frontier institution, the mission also served to prepare Indians for secular, albeit economic, participation in Spanish colonial society. At the mission neophytes learned different techniques of masonry and carpentry, skills which would prove useful in the construction of the church, convento, and related structures. Generally, Old World farming methods and husbandry formed part of the mission curriculum. To the missionary, nonetheless, the most important role of the mission program was the Christian salvation of the natives. In the *doctrina*, where religious instruction took place, friars prepared their charges for baptism, penance, Holy Communion, matrimony and sometimes confirmation. Converted Mexican Indians often assisted a lone friar in his work. The missionaries' hope, that the mission Indians would one day enter the Congregation of the Faithful as full-fledged Roman Catholics, was for them never fully realized. Instead, the Franciscans learned, sometimes after years of attempted conversions, that the Indians accepted from Christianity whatever would be useful for them but did not relinquish the beliefs of their ancestors.

Neophytes were often caught between the Spanish friar and their Indians priests. At Pecos, as in other pueblos, the mission resulted in a crisis. Generally, Indians viewed Christianity and Spanish culture as threats against the "old ways" of life and as sources of resentment throughout the Pueblo world. Yet the undeniable fact of the relationship between Franciscan friar and neophyte was that the pueblo was the single most important component of the mission. In seventeenth-century New Mexico, without the pueblo there would have been no mission. The Pueblo world had begun to evaluate that and other relationships with Spaniards.

Spanish-Indian relationships were not exclusively antagonistic. In the eighty years since Oñate's establishment of New Mexico, intermarriages and religious kinships had been established. Friendships and social associations had been formed among Spanish frontiersmen and their Indian counterparts. But such relationships were not enough to thwart Indian resentment against the injustices of Spanish colonialism. Long-standing grievances caused by an oppressive colonial economic system and a suppressive Indian policy which worked to undermine the religious, political, and social traditions of the Pueblos reached the breaking point between 1675 and 1680. Out of the turmoil emerged an Indian leader known to the Spaniards as Popé. He would lead a revolt unlike any New Mexicans had ever experienced. He would put to the test whatever relationships existed among them.

Popé organized his revolt by uniting the northern Pueblos and Apaches in a military alliance against the Spaniards. Sworn to secrecy, the pueblos waited for the signal to rebel on an appointed day in August 1680. The pro-Spanish factions at each pueblo thought differently about the planned revolt and began to warn their Hispanic friends and relatives. The situation at Pecos was similarly ambivalent despite the hostility of the anti-Spanish faction which clamored for vengeance, especially in the case of Maese de Campo Francisco Javier. Shortly before the general uprising, Javier had seized a number of Apaches at Pecos who were under his protection. Having distributed some of his captives among his followers, he had the rest sent to Parral for sale. The Pecos, who depended on Apache trade, were outraged. For them the planned revolt would take on a more immediate reason for revenge. When the revolt broke on August 10, 1680, the Pecos spared their minister, Fray Fernando de Velasco. The pro-Spanish faction intervened and permitted his safe passage out of the pueblo. But Velasco's subordinate, Fray Juan de la Pedrosa, and at least one Spanish family were put to death by the rebelling Pecos. Later, the hapless Friar Velasco and several of his brethren were killed by rebels at Galisteo, southwest of Pecos. The situation was similar at other pueblos though some Spaniards were spared and their Indian friends fled with them. Death and devastation became widespread throughout the province.

Meanwhile, a large force of Pueblo warriors had laid siege to Santa Fe, the provincial capital. Riding their horses close enough for the Spaniards to hear them, Pecos warriors demanded revenge over the Javier affair. "Give us Francisco Javier, who is the reason we have risen, and we will remain in peace as before," they shouted. The siege lasted a week during which time the Spaniards, under Governor Antonio Otermín, counterattacked but were forced back into the walled villa of Santa Fe. Finally, after their water supply had been cut off by the warriors, the Spaniards were forced to flee the capital. More than a thousand people eventually

PECOS—GATEWAY TO PUEBLOS & PLAINS

After years of political hardship, and famine and drought attributed to Spanish interference in the natural order of things, the Pueblos erupted on the morning of August 10, 1680. At Pecos, the huge church was burned and its massive walls torn apart. The priest was killed on his way to warn others of the revolt.

PECOS MISSION IN THE SEVENTEENTH CENTURY

For a few brief years, the Pecos escaped the Spanish presence. They built a kiva in the ruined convent as a symbol
of a return to the days before the Spanish altered their lives.

gathered at El Paso del Norte-now a community of refugees from the Pueblo Revolt. After they had overcome their grief and the traumatic events of recent days, the Spaniards called a council of war, the first of many, and planned to retake New Mexico.

Twelve years would pass before the Spaniards could negotiate their return with the leaders of a failing Pueblo alliance in revolt. Still, the Spaniards would have to deal with resistance. In 1541, Fray Luis de Úbeda could have told them all about Indian resistance.

IX PECOS IN THE EIGHTEENTH CENTURY
JOSEPH P. SANCHEZ

ON JANUARY 1, 1829, Father Juan Felipe Ortiz, a diocesan priest from Santa Fe, began a new administration at Pecos Mission. He was the first non-Franciscan ever to do so. That day, the Franciscan ministry at Pecos came to an end after a long history which had begun in 1541. The summer before Father Ortiz arrived, Fray José Castro had baptized the last Franciscan-tutored Indian at Pecos. As the aged Fray José left the partially ruined mission church and poverty-stricken Indian pueblo, he must have felt a certain sorrow, for he not only caught a glimpse of Pecos's future, he knew its past. Much had happened at Pecos in the 148 years after the Pueblo Revolt. Between 1692 and 1828, both pueblo and mission fell into decline, and despite some good fortunes, both failed in the end. The last act in the drama at Pecos began with a reconciliation between Spaniards and Puebloans, who had been at war from 1680 until 1692.

Summer 1692: Governor Don Diego de Vargas led a small army northward along the Río Grande from El Paso to Santa Fe. His objective was to retake New Mexico from Indian rebels who had held the province since 1680. The march up the Río Grande to Sandia Pueblo was uneventful primarily because all the pueblos south of there had been abandoned years before. Consequently, no Indians were seen by the Spaniards. By mid-September Vargas had laid siege to Santa Fe, and before nightfall of the first day, the natives had surrendered without a fight. The next day Spanish priests absolved the rebel Indians of their apostasy, and children, most of whom had been born after the Pueblo Revolt, were presented for baptism. With the aid of Luis Túpatu, the most powerful of the rebel chieftains, Don Diego was able to persuade many of the pueblos near Santa Fe to submit to Spanish sovereignty once again.

Meanwhile, at Pecos, mounted Indian messengers warned their people that the Spaniards were coming. When Vargas arrived at the old pueblo, he found it abandoned, and in five days he could not induce its inhabitants to return. In the hope of convincing the Pecos that he came in peace, Vargas took captives and released them so that they could tell their people of his peaceful intentions. From the captives the Spaniards learned that the Pecos were divided over accepting their

friendly entreaties. As before, a pro-Spanish faction desired peace, but the anti-Spanish faction, comprised mostly of young warriors, opposed them. Unable to unite the two groups, the Pueblo leaders decided to abandon Pecos. Still, the Spaniards hoped to induce them to return. Before withdrawing his army, the sage Vargas ordered a large cross erected in the pueblo's plaza. As a sign of amity, his soldiers painted crosses on some of the house walls. In a conspicuous place, a small cross with a piece of paper to be carried for safe conduct by any of the Pecos Indians who wished to discuss peace, was left behind. Then, without disturbing anything in the pueblo, Vargas and his troops left.

Three weeks later Vargas and his small army returned to Pecos. The governor sent two Indian youths to deliver his message once again. He wanted peace; he expected them to submit peacefully. Should the Pecos decide to fight, however, Vargas and his Indian allies would oblige them.

Reminiscent of their ancestors who had watched conquering Spanish armies approach their walls, the Pecos, standing on their roof tops, peered into the distance and saw the Spaniards and their auxiliary Indian force march toward them along a meandering trail. This time it was different. When Vargas and his cohorts finally reached the pueblo, its entrance was crowded by Pecoseños who held branches of evergreens over their heads. At mid-afternoon on Friday, October 17, 1692, the two peoples embraced one another in reconciliation. Around a large cross, which the Pecos had erected as a sign of peace, the Indians chanted "Alabado sea Dios y Su

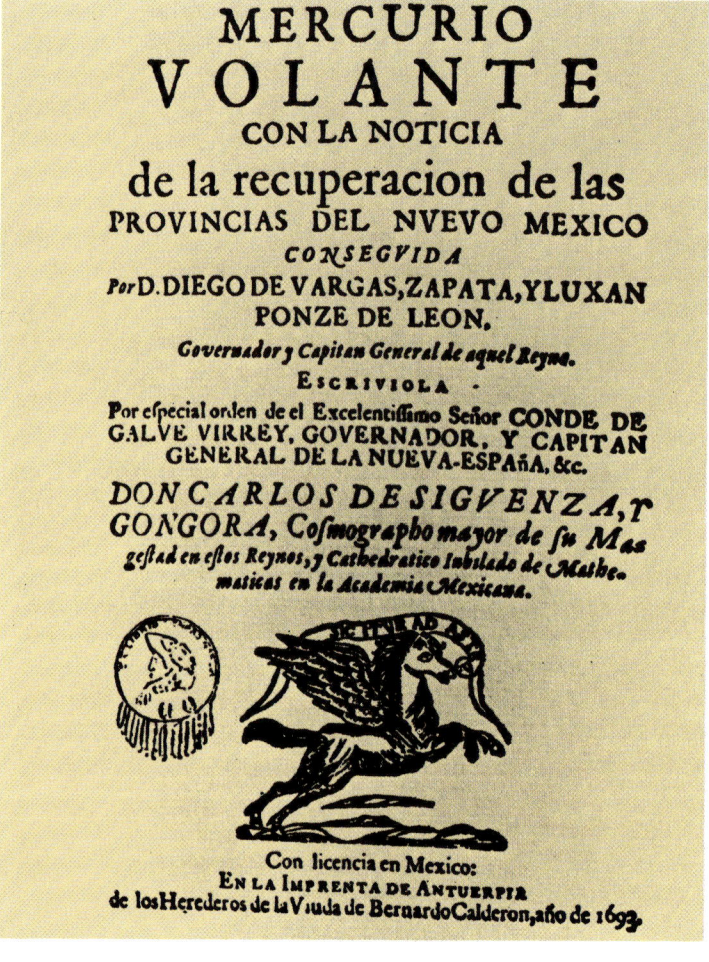

"Mercurio Volante," published in 1693 by don Carlos de Sigüenza y Góngora, recounted the history of de Varga's reconquest of New Mexico.

Santísimo Sacramento"—Praised be God and His Most Holy Sacrament. With like incantations the Spaniards responded.

As the sun descended in the late afternoon, the cool fall air brought Spaniard and Indian closer around the campfires. Soldiers, holding their capes around them for warmth, and Indians, bundled in their buffalo robes, became spectators to their own pageantry. While a squad of soldiers stood with their swords unsheathed, Governor Vargas ordered an ensign to raise the royal banner three times. Each time the banner went up the crowd shouted "Long live the King, Don Carlos the second, may God spare him, King of Spain and of all this kingdom and its lands and pueblos, and these natives who are his vassals!" When the soldiers threw their hats in the air, the cheering Indians likewise tossed up their robes in jubilation. Then, as at the other pueblos which had submitted to Vargas, the Pecos brought out their children born since 1680 for baptism. That night, the Pecos cautiously embraced Spanish sovereignty, once again.

After the tumultuous first decade of the resettlement of New Mexico, affairs between Indian and Spaniard fell into the usual pattern of colonialism. Although the friars had returned to New Mexico, one aspect of the old colonialism did not survive the revolt: the *encomienda*, by which certain Spaniards collected tribute from Indians. If the Pueblo Revolt had not succeeded in completely forcing out the Spaniards, it had, at least, caused the abolition of tribute collection under the *encomienda*. The *encomendero*, who traditionally had offered the pueblos military protection in

Retablo, Our Lady of Guadalupe, ca. 1795–1820. Our Lady represented the appearance of the Virgin Mary in the New World and remains one of the most popular religious figures.

PECOS IN THE EIGHTEENTH CENTURY

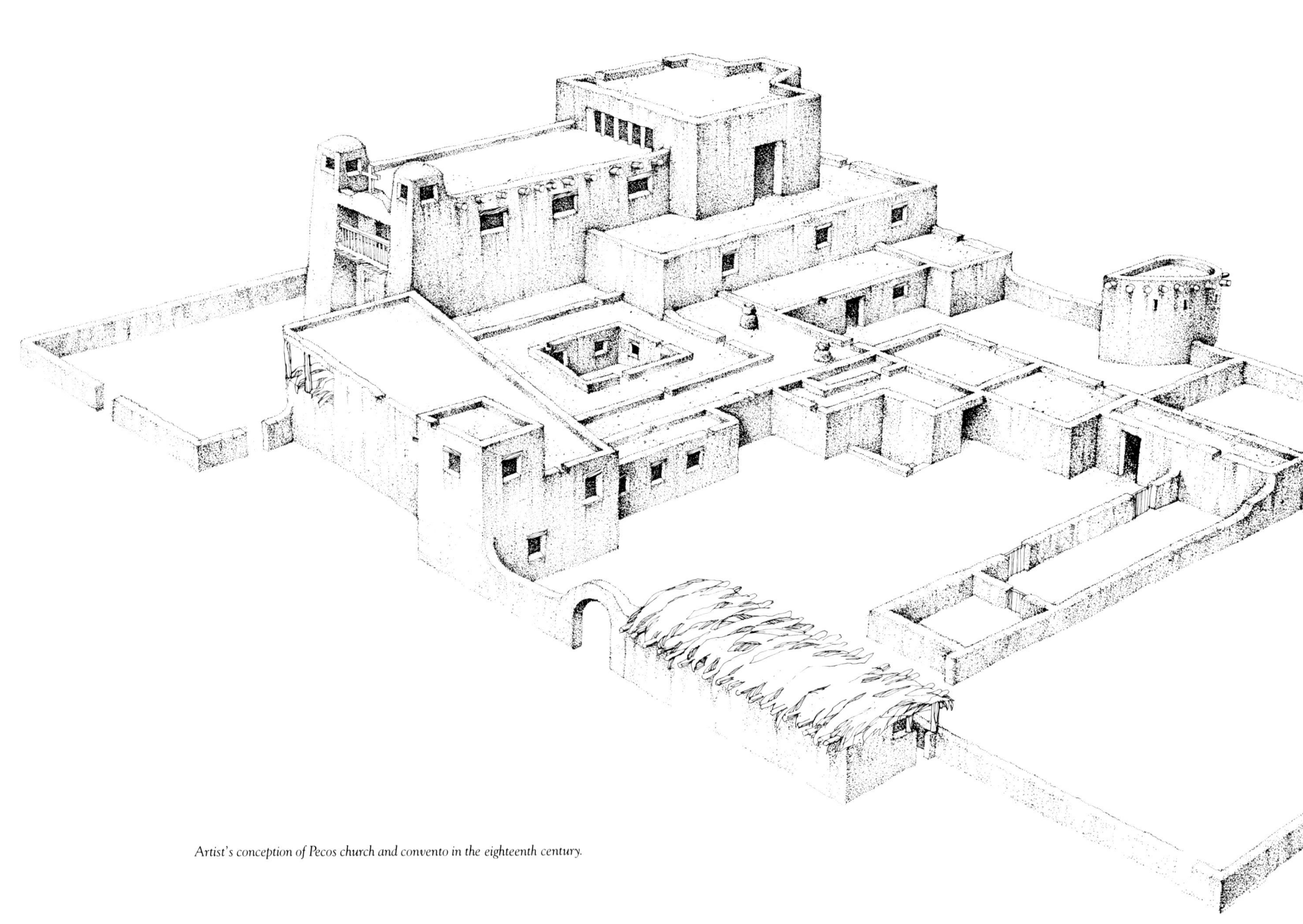

Artist's conception of Pecos church and convento in the eighteenth century.

exchange for tribute, was now replaced by a presidial guard which would defend New Mexico at the expense of the provincial treasury.

Following the Reconquista by Diego de Vargas, the Pecos witnessed the return of the Franciscans. Fray Diego de Zeinos began the reconstruction of the church at Pecos over the ruins of the old church, which had been destroyed in the 1680 Revolt. Before the first year was over, Fray Diego had baptized 103 Indians, mostly infants and children. Although Father Zeinos was an ideal missionary, a fateful accident cut short his ministry at Pecos. One day Zeinos picked up an harquebus and the weapon discharged, killing a Pecos servant who happened by. To avoid trouble Spanish officials quickly removed Zeinos from Pecos. During the investigation of the incident, however, the Pecos Indians sent a delegation to plead for Father Zeinos's return to Pecos. But Spanish officials instead assigned another friar to Pecos.

Another two decades would pass before the church at Pecos had a completed appearance. In those twenty years, much had changed at Pecos. Sixteen friars had come and gone, each leaving his imprint in the minds and lore of the people he served. Perhaps the greatest change affecting Pecos was an increase in Apache raids, which had been caused partly by the advance of aggressive Comanches moving down the east side of the Rockies into former Apache country. Furthermore, Apaches had never forgotten that Pecos warriors joined Diego de Vargas in the Sandia Mountain campaign (1704-1706) against them. By 1716 the Spaniards were embroiled in a full-scale war against Apache and Comanche raiders; and their Pueblo allies nearest the plains, such as Taos, Picuris, Pecos, and Galisteo, bore the brunt of Plains Indian offensives.

By the mid-1700s, the Comanche threat to the Province of New Mexico was at its peak. In 1745 Pecos had suffered a serious blow when Comanche raiders killed twelve people there. Shortly afterwards, the Pecos, braving the danger of marauding Comanche warriors who watched the trails to Santa Fe, journeyed to the provincial capital to petition the Spanish governor for permission to enter the Great Plains for their annual buffalo hunt. License granted, the Pecos organized a large party of nearly all of their warriors for the hunt. Once on the Plains, Comanche scouts dogged them for some distance. Despite their diligence, the Pecos walked into a Comanche ambush and were routed with many casualties. The Comanche were relentless in their attacks against Indian pueblo and Spanish settlement. In the winter of 1748 Comanches mounted a series of raids. At Pecos thirteen Puebloans were killed before the raiders were driven away. The Comanches had practically brought the New Mexican province to a standstill.

In 1750 the innovative Governor Tomás Vélez Cachupín visited Pecos and to his surprise discovered many of the Carlana, Paloma, and Cuartelejo Apaches living there in peace. Noting the influence of the Pecos on the nomadic groups, Governor Vélez encouraged others to settle among the Pecoseños, a move which

In the Sangre de Cristo Mountains above Pecos, the tall ponderosa pine mix with Engelmann spruce and aspen. Their straight, strong trunks have been used as building materials in the valley from early pueblo times.

would improve the old pueblo's defense against marauding nomads. The defenses at Galisteo were likewise improved. Next, he attempted to make peace with the Comanches who had displaced the Apaches at Taos. In July 1751, the governor met with Comanches at Taos and attempted to befriend them; but, as he learned four months later it was to no avail. In November Comanches attacked Galisteo but were repulsed. Governor Vélez, tempted to carry out a punitive expedition against them, decided instead to use diplomacy. During the winter of 1751-1752, Vélez formed a number of alliances with Apache groups to keep the Comanches at bay. The method worked until the late 1750s, when Vélez's successor broke the alliances and Comanches took to raiding again.

For the next decade Comanche raiders posed a serious threat to the survival of New Mexico. Finally, after years of a trial-and-error Comanche policy, Governor Juan Bautista de Anza (1778-1787) waged war against Comanches, who suddenly in 1785 asked for peace.

Toward the end of the 1700s, Pecos, beset with a host of economic problems and ravaged by a smallpox epidemic, went into a steep decline from which it was never able to recover. Besieged by Comanches for decades, the Pecoseños found it too hazardous to farm the bottomlands along the Pecos River. Gradually, they were forced to farm small plots closer to their homes. When, in 1794, Spanish settlers moved into the area and founded the village of San Miguel del Vado, the death knell for Pecos was sounded. San Miguel soon displaced Pecos as the trade center. At the beginning of the nineteenth century Pecos stood on the threshold of oblivion.

NO ONE EVER KNEW just how many Comanches there were, but they numbered in the thousands—fewer than guessed at the height of their wars, but so many as to hinder any cohesive organization. They counted themselves as numerous as the stars, a vast set of proud, autonomous individuals, none bound to accept any authority higher than himself except by his own choice. The nation emerged from the Rocky Mountains of present Wyoming and northern Colorado in the dawn of the eighteenth century: small groups of Shoshonean-speaking families, lured by horses then spreading from New Mexico to transform Indian lives on the neighboring Plains.

Of all the Indian peoples caught up in the equestrian revolution, none adapted more swiftly or completely than the Comanches, who would build a new pastoral society around the horse. As their mobility and their prowess in war and hunting grew, they clustered in larger bands. Still, the nomadic Comanches functioned with minimal political structure, bound by speech and

PECOS — GATEWAY TO PUEBLOS & PLAINS

Glorieta Pass—a "corridor to other worlds." Beyond it lay the Río Grande Valley and Santa Fe—
the seat of government that even the wandering Comanche had to reckon with.

customs, deeply conscious of their likeness and likemindedness as Comanches and of their supremacy within the expanding vastness of the Comanchería. (The term "Comanchería" may refer either to the Comanche people as a whole or, in this instance, to their territory.)

The Comanche nation comprised three major divisions in the eighteenth century: Yupes and Yamparicas, who ranged mostly northward from the Arkansas River, and Cuchanecs, who ranged increasingly southward. Their flexible structure adapted readily to movements of the buffalo and changing necessities of protection and warfare. The amorphous, composite bands changed in size and leadership as situations changed. Successful leaders attracted larger numbers; groups troubled by deficient leadership tended to fade away. Always the basic unit of Comanche life was the family camp, each with its own headman, who advised rather than commanded. One family headman emerged as head chief of the band; all of them together constituted an advisory council, chaired by the head chief.

Warriors tended to obey decisions of the council, but nomadic life made it impossible for chiefs always to keep in touch with their warriors or even to know whether their policies were honored. Usually, offenders were merely rebuked or admonished. In theory, at least, any warrior could lead a war or raiding party, and no power could curb him: he simply announced his intention, and if he had a favorable reputation, others rallied to his venture. Possible gains of booty, especially horses, and of glory were ample incentives.

Vengeance was a Comanche imperative. A parent who lost a son to the enemy could never rest content without an enemy scalp to even the score. A bereaved father or brother of fighting age could lead a vengeance party or seek a scalp alone. An older parent with no son left could ask some warrior to avenge the lost son, which no honorable man could refuse. The loss of a distinguished chief or some grave affront to the honor of the band could spark an extended, bitter vendetta, requiring many scalps and horses in recompense.

Comanches first came to Pecos in the 1730s as strangers seeking vengeance. Perhaps their initial target was several Apaches, their mortal enemies, then sheltered within the pueblo; perhaps they were reacting to injuries inflicted by Pecos warriors during New Mexican expeditions against Comanche marauders; perhaps Comanche and Pecos hunters had clashed on the buffalo plains. Whatever the provocation, once caught up in Comanche vendettas, Pecos knew no security of lives or property until New Mexico attained peace with them.

Understanding was the key to peace. At midcentury, provincial Governor Tomás Vélez Cachupín studied the Comanches as diligently as he strengthened defenses against them. He learned that Comanches did not function as a single nation, that there were countless groups with their own chiefs, each acting upon his own inclination. Some held particular grievances, which sparked such attacks as Pecos suffered. Others were peaceable and restrained their followers from wrongdoing. To break the cycle of vengeance and raiding required correct identification and exemplary punishment of actual wrongdoers; indiscriminate war against all Comanches only spawned new vendettas. Moreover, to conciliate them, the frequent abuses they suffered in New Mexico must be curbed.

That approach worked. In autumn 1751, Vélez Cachupín pursued and decisively defeated a large Comanche party that had attacked Pecos. He sent survivors back to the Comanchería with his invitation to make peace and his promise to drub any future offenders. The Comanche leaders agreed that it would be better to stop the wars and make the most of the profitable trade fairs at Taos. Within the year they celebrated a peace with New Mexico that endured as long as Vélez Cachupín managed its complexities. He personally supervised the Comanche trade, ensuring that neither settlers nor pueblos mistreated them, protecting their camps from theft and extortion, and promptly adjudicating disputes. Such fairness and courtesy won Comanche confidence.

The peace broke down in the eight-year interval between the two terms of Vélez Cachupín, was quickly restored upon his return, then collapsed again after his final departure in 1767. But his successes demonstrated both the advantages and the practicability of peace between Comanches and New Mexicans. Permanent alliance with the Comanches became a prime objective of Spanish frontier policy.

Definitive peace evolved only after 1779, when New Mexican forces led by Governor Juan Bautista de Anza vanquished the leaders of a long, fierce Comanche feud against the province. Depredations virtually ceased after that, but Anza would entertain no treaty talks until all the bands would unite to seek a peace binding upon all Comanches and all Spaniards. That was hard for a far-flung nation with such fragmentary organization, but by 1785 the Comanches wanted peace badly enough to try. That autumn Chief Ecueracapa called all Comanches to the Arkansas River to decide the question of tribal peace, and was authorized to negotiate binding terms with Anza. The chief channeled his overture through Pecos, and thirteen Pecos delegates helped carry back to Ecueracapa's camp Governor Anza's response to his peace proposal. Enthusiasm on all sides swiftly carried the process to climax in a treaty ceremony at Pecos in February 1786. Meanwhile, the easternmost Comanches negotiated peace at the Texas capital, San Antonio.

Why did the Comanches forge their new link with New Mexico at Pecos? Perhaps Taos symbolized too many old grievances; perhaps Pecos seemed more convenient as Comanches shifted ever southward. Certainly Pecos afforded them handier access to Santa Fe, with less exposure to enemies en route.

From 1786 onwards, Comanches peacefully frequented Pecos: sometimes in hundreds, for whom officially supervised trade fairs were held, but also, increasingly over the years, in casual little groups visiting and trading at their convenience. Women and children came routinely, a sign of Comanche confidence in the peace. While their followers camped near Pecos, leaders often rode on the Santa Fe to visit the governor, reaffirming their friendship and transacting business.

COMANCHES & PECOS

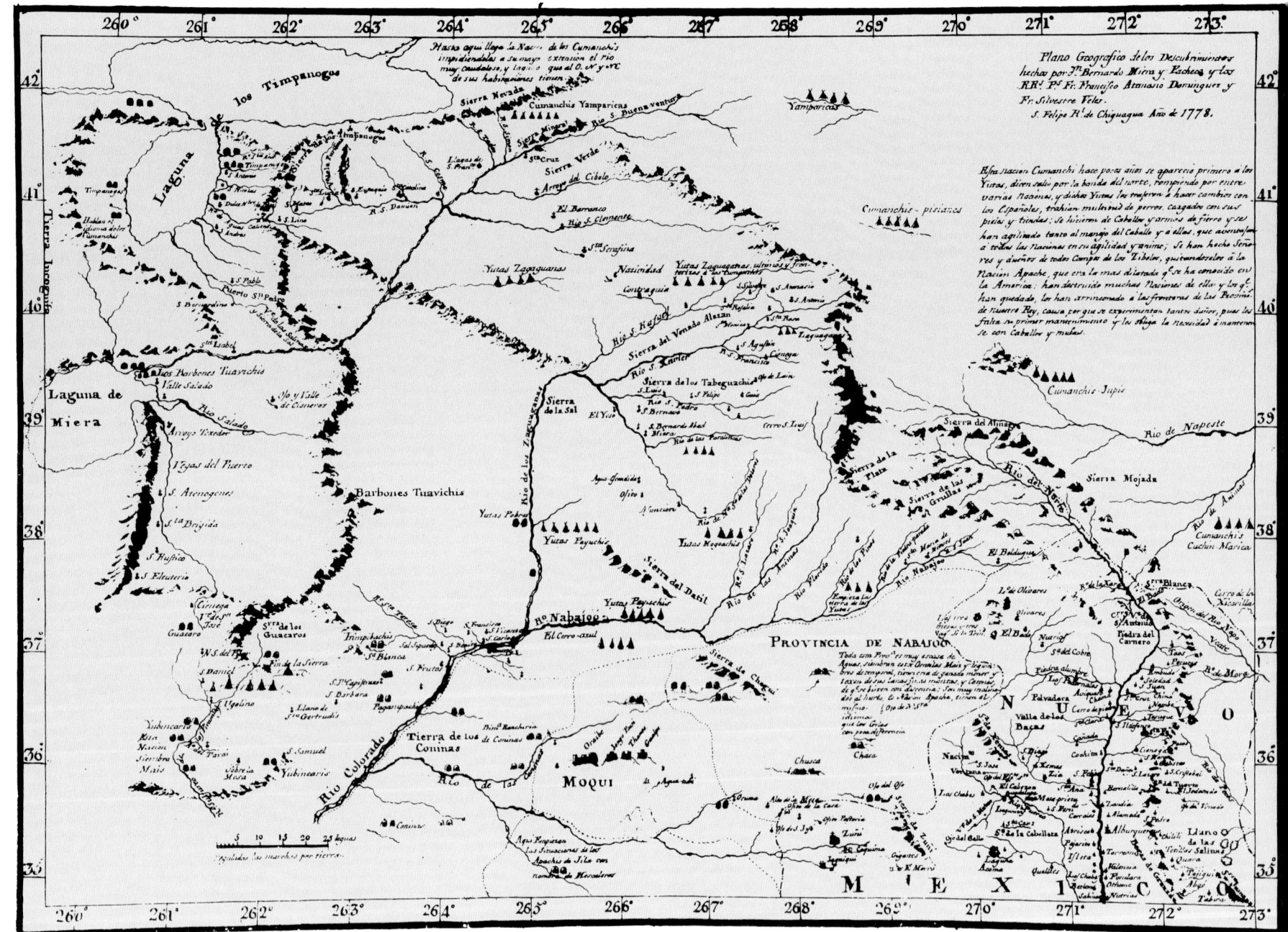

Based on a regional map by Bernardo Miera Y Pacheco, this 1778 map delineates Indian concentrations.
Comanches are heavily indicated on the eastern side of the Rocky Mountains.

Reciprocal hospitality awaited New Mexican visitors to the Comanchería. Once certain of the peace, Hispanic and Pueblo hunters and traders ventured regularly to the Comanchería.

Much of the trade reiterated patterns ancient at Pecos: wandering plainsfolk exchanging hides, meat, tallow, and captives for Pueblo agricultural produce and manufactures. Comanches readily fitted into such mutually advantageous patterns of trade and friendship, as Hispanic settlers had done before them. But the numerous Comanches, empowered by the horse, supplied quantities far exceeding local consumption, and the overplus swelled New Mexican exports southward to neighboring provinces. In turn, the Comanches gained a nice array of manufactures from New Spain and Europe: cotton and woolen textiles, metal implements and weapons, clothing and ornaments.

Comanche women generated much of the new prosperity. Their men's success in the hunt meant little in the marketplace until skillful wives jerked the meat, rendered the tallow, and tanned the hides. In return, they gained kettles and knives, fabrics and needles, buttons and beads, mirrors and combs, which eased women's work, enhanced their productivity and status, and embellished their crafts. Such accumulations were manageable now that horses transported Comanche households from campsite to campsite.

In fact, horses made possible all the new affluence, and were themselves prime currency throughout the Comanchería and on adjacent frontiers. Through occasional purchase and frequent theft of animals, and increasingly through capture from wild herds and breeding of their own stock, within their first equestrian century Comanches developed horse herds of legendary numbers and quality. That attracted more and more traders to the Comanchería, thus diminishing Comanche reliance upon such marts as Pecos.

But Comanche ascendancy was short-lived. The final dwindling and abandonment of Pecos coincided with a surge of woes in the Comanchería: a devastating smallpox epidemic in 1816; the breakdown of the eastern Comanches' trade connection in Hispanic Texas amidst the turmoils of revolution; and mounting tensions with the Anglo-Texans who would become their nemesis. Within four decades after the demise of Pecos, the Comanche world also collapsed. The survivors bowed to reservation life in present southwestern Oklahoma, where the tribal roll now lists some 6,000 Comanches.

XI ANATOMY OF AN ABANDONMENT
ALBERT H. SCHROEDER

ABANDONMENT OF PECOS PUEBLO

was a 150-year ordeal marked by a series of events that brought about final desertion of the site in 1838-1840. It began with the Pueblo Revolt of 1680-1692 in which Pecos took an active part against the Spaniards, only to turn friendly in 1693, but not completely so.

This shift in alliance led to factional disputes within the pueblo. During the rebellion of 1696, a Jemez Indian, an active leader in the revolt, came to Pecos where he was received by Don Diego, leader of the rebel Pecos faction. In a meeting that followed, Don Felipe, the governor of Pecos, objected to Diego's attempt to lead the pueblo into the revolt, and Diego was taken out and hanged.

Continuous trouble was evident into 1700 between Felipe and the friends and relatives of the rebellious ringleader of 1696. Several hostile acts occurred in late 1700, and the anti-Spanish faction was jailed in Santa Fe, but later escaped into the mountains and joined Jicarilla Apaches; yet Pecos continued to be divided. Some members of the opposition group reached the point of requesting permission to move to Pojoaque Pueblo north of Santa Fe. Judging by the decrease in the population of Pecos, from about 1,500 at the end of the 1692 rebellion to between 700 and 800 in the middle 1690s, some type of separation seems to have taken place if no other factor such as an epidemic was involved.

Already weakened by the probable departure of the opposition, Pecos suffered a second cultural shock when mounted Comanches in 1706 appeared in northeastern New Mexico. They worked their way south to the Canadian River east of Pecos by 1715, driving the Apaches of the area south towards Texas. In addition to raids on the pueblo, these Comanches stood as a constant threat to Pecos bison hunting parties on the plains. Many of the Pecos during this period also served as auxiliaries on Spanish campaigns. Deaths resulting from these conflicts led to additional population losses at Pecos, but probably were not sufficient to account for the total decrease of about 200 to 521 people by 1730.

Perhaps unreported epidemics also were in part responsible for the lower population figure. Several occurred only a few years later: smallpox in 1738 and

The population at Pecos gradually diminished over the centuries. Many died, some drifted away, but the pueblo is not dead. The place and the people have simply parted company.

another epidemic in 1748 which combined probably played a major part in further reducing the population figure by another 200 to the middle 300s by the 1760s. Epidemics in the 1770s decreased the number to the middle 200s. Following the 1786 peace that the Spaniards negotiated with Comanches, the Pecos population remained fairly stable, in the middle 100s, until the end of the century.

Without the above figures, the reduction over the years in the number of kivas reported in use at any one time—sixteen in 1591, many in 1692, but only four mentioned in 1714 when the Spaniards were destroying all kivas in the Pueblo world—would indicate either an unexplained loss in individual kiva membership or a general depopulation through time. Obviously, the documented figures indicate a serious loss among the Pecos.

The presence of so few kivas in the late 1600s and early 1700s indicates a major disruption in the way of life at the pueblo. The construction of the South Pueblo close to the mission church during this period may well be an architectural reflection of this situation. The apparent lack of an associated kiva, plus Indian-made Spanish ceramic forms and candle holders recovered from the South Pueblo, seem also to support the belief that this structure was built by the Christian Indians.

The combination of factional splits and withdrawals, losses during wars and while hunting on the plains, and deaths due to epidemics during the 1700s undoubtedly left gaps in a variety of socio-religious activities. Societies and ceremonies must have been seriously handicapped. The depletion was so great by the end of the 1700s that even the church no longer assigned a resident priest to Pecos, and it was reduced to the status of a *visita*.

In the early 1800s, Spaniards along the Río Grande began to move east and establish themselves along the Pecos River below Pecos Pueblo at San José and San Miguel del Vado. The church had trained Pecos Indians to make various items the Spaniards needed. As the Spaniards settled on the Pecos, some of the inhabitants of the dying pueblo, numbering only thirty families in 1812, moved to San Miguel to pursue their crafts. Names of these Indians are recorded in the non-pueblo church records of this town. The last baptism at Pecos took place in June 1828.

When the Santa Fe Trail caravans first crossed westward over the plains in 1821 and trudged past the pueblo, the survivors at Pecos were huddled in a few rooms in and around the north end of the quadrangle. In places the pueblo still stood three stories high with ladders leading to wooden galleries or walkways on each upper level. However, the opening of the Santa Fe Trail and its economic effect on New Mexico came too late to play a part in any revival at Pecos. The remnant that hung on, seventeen to twenty people, in number, deserted the ancient home, most of them moving out together to live with their linguistic relatives at Jemez Pueblo in the 1838-1840 period. The last of these survivors, Augustín Pecos, died at Jemez in 1919.

Various traditions and tales relate to the abandonment of Pecos, such as those of the Pecos waiting for the

Nuestra Señora de Los Ángeles (Our Lady of the Angels), by eighteenth century painter Juan Correa, hung in the Pecos church for 100 years. Her care was entrusted to the village of Pecos who return Her to the mission for Mass every August.

return of Montezuma to lead them, a serpent god to which humans were sacrificed, and a perpetual fire that should not die out which otherwise would bring the downfall of the pueblo. Only the last seems to have some basis in fact.

In 1591, the journal recounting Castaño de Sosa's visit of that year describes the kivas at Pecos and stated "they make no fire inside, because they bring many coals from without and they are covered with ashes more neatly than I can describe." Josiah Gregg wrote that he "beheld a consecrated fire, silently smoldering under a cover of ashes, in the basin of a small altar" in one of the kivas. Adolf Bandelier's Pecos informant in 1880 stated that "the sacred embers were maintained in one specific room of the pueblo." It would seem that the ash pit adjacent to the hearth in pueblo kivas might have served as a container of ash from a previous fire to cover embers of the new fire (to represent continuity?) brought in from the "perpetual fire."

After the fires at Pecos died out and its people left, exposure to the elements, neglect, and vandalism gradually brought down the walls to form a crumpled blanket over the village.

XII RÍO PECOS UNDER THE MEXICAN EAGLE
FELIX D. ALMARÁZ, JR.

THE LONG TENURE OF SPANISH

colonial rule in New Mexico ended silently in 1821 when the news of Mexican independence arrived in Santa Fe the day after Christmas. Notwithstanding political modification at the top of the social pyramid, Mexican independence hardly touched the inhabitants who lived in the Río Grande–Río Pecos watersheds. Their culture, laws, language, land grants, religion, customs, and traditions continued seemingly undisturbed as the eagle, symbol of a different sovereignty, descended upon New Mexico.

Mexican nationhood signified a more flexible policy of frontier control. Independence meant the removal of restrictive barriers against commerce with Anglo Americans. On September 1, 1821, a Missouri merchant, William Becknell, left Arrow Rock, Missouri, with a pack train of merchandise and a party of about twenty companions on a westward trek to Santa Fe. By mid-November the Becknell party entered New Mexico via the upper Pecos River Valley. At Santa Fe they enjoyed a

cordial reception extended by government officials. More enjoyable was the thriving business they conducted, selling their cargo to avid buyers. The following year Becknell repeated the overland crossing, this time with heavy wagons loaded with trade goods, and reaped a sizable profit. His success opened the border to a steady migration of wagon trains to New Mexico along the rut-marked Santa Fe Trail.

The arrival of the Missouri traders caused New Mexicans to shift their reliance from Chihuahua merchants to Anglo American suppliers. In the former relationship Hispanics exerted little influence upon market conditions; in the latter contact their economic situation improved appreciably because American traders sought favorable acceptance and accommodation in northern New Mexico.

In accordance with land laws enacted during this period, the alienation of pueblo communal properties gathered momentum. Southeast of Santa Fe, for example, Hispanic settlers petitioned the territorial government to award to them vacant lands adjacent to the Río Pecos, above and below the ancient Indian pueblo. Concerning Indian property rights, the demarcation of village boundaries (as accomplished in 1815) was not equivalent to guaranteed possession of title.

In 1824, Governor Bartolomé Baca and the Provincial Deputation yielded to rising pressures for grants in productive fields by lowering legal barriers protecting native ancestral lands. Regardless of restrictions of law, Hispanic settlers in the Río Pecos region began to cultivate unused agricultural lands. Rafael Benavides requested multiple land grants for himself and his friends. Another petitioner, also named Benavides (Luis, a retired soldier), applied for a modest grant of Pecos land to cultivate maize and wheat to supplement the meals of his large family. Throughout the remainder of the 1820s, dozens of Hispanic families occupied vacant lands in the vicinity of *el cañón de Pecos*. Simply by tilling the soil the Hispanics, many of whom resided elsewhere, indicated their determination to retain their claims.

Communities situated near the Río Pecos stretched out for a distance of twenty miles above and below the Indian pueblo. Starting with Cañón de Pecos at the northern end, the towns, like colorful beads on a loose strand, accented the riverbanks and lent descriptive names to the landscape—Los Trigos, Las Ruedas, El Gusano, San José del Vado, and San Miguel del Vado.

Indicative of the rise and decline of population within a quarter century, the 1794 census disclosed 165 Indians residing at Pecos, whereas El Vado was virtually empty. Twenty-five years later (1820), the population of Pecos dropped to fifty-eight but El Vado district boasted 735 settlers. By 1825, an itinerant Franciscan recorded one baptism at Pecos compared to 176 for El Vado; in marriages, one at Pecos and forty in El Vado; and in burials, one at Pecos and ninety-four at El Vado.

Of the two communities forming El Vado district, San Miguel became the town that glowed like a bright beacon in the first half of the nineteenth century. Initially settled by Hispanics from the environs of Santa

Fe, with the help of a few Indians from Pecos and even fewer *mestizos*,* by 1803 it received formal recognition as a full-fledged civil settlement. As more colonists arrived, a minority of whom were genízaros, a myth evolved about San Miguel del Vado being a *genízaro*† community. Regardless of the myth, two geographic features attracted settlers to San Miguel: the availability of fertile land adjoining two riverbanks, and the location of a convenient river ford.

Politically, San Miguel del Vado assumed added importance when the Mexican government designated the town as a customs collecting depot. Although in actual practice freighters paid customs duties to authorities in Santa Fe, the hamlet of San Miguel del Vado remained the official port of entry until 1843. On his initial sojourn to New Mexico, Josiah Gregg recorded in his journal a description of San Miguel del Vado, which he said

> consisted of irregular clusters of mud-walled huts, and is situated in the fertile valley of Río Pecos, a silvery little river which ripples from the snowy mountains of Santa Fe—from which this frontier village is nearly fifty miles to the southwest [sic]. The road makes this great southern bend, to find a passageway through the broken extremity of the spur of mountains . . . which from this point south is cut up into detached ridges and table plains. . . .

Another observer in 1821 commented that San Miguel comprised "a hundred houses, a large church, and two miserably constructed flour mills. . . ."

As the decade of the 1820s ended, Friar José de Castro concluded his ministry in the del Vado district and the visiting responsibility at Nuestra Señora de los Ángeles at Pecos. Prior to his departure, the Franciscan transferred statistical church records to a diocesan priest from Santa Fe.

In 1833, the Bishop of Durango, José Antonio Laureano López de Zubiría y Escalante, toured the northern communities of Christian worship in New Mexico. When the bishop visited San Miguel del Vado, the impoverished condition of the parish church shocked him. A logical explanation, of course, was that the circuit-riding priest from Santa Fe assigned greater priority to preaching the Gospel at remote ranchos and hamlets than to physical maintenance of church buildings. The records of his itinerant ministry reflected the attention given to outlying congregations. Even so, appalled at what he surveyed at San Miguel del Vado, Bishop Zubiría refrained from commenting on the Pecos mission.

Owing to the compactness of the Río Pecos Valley, combined with adequate rainfall in the highlands, the type of agriculture Hispanic and Indian settlers practiced was irrigation farming along alluvial terraces. The enterprise involved local government supervision and private initiative in building control *presas* (dams) to conserve runoff, and in the construction of secondary diversion watergates and lateral canals. Whenever rainfall was ample, farmers might draw whatever amount

---

*Mestizo: an offspring of the union of a Hispanic and an Indian.
†Genízaro: a ransomed Christian Indian who adopted a Hispanic life style; also a ransomed Hispanic captive who involuntarily or otherwise lived among Indians for an extended period of time.

their alluvial fields required; in times of scarcity the irrigation *mayordomo* (overseer) determined the ration of water.

In areas of the valley where bottomlands attracted settlers, the irrigation system varied somewhat, with local government sponsoring excavation of an *acequia madre* (main canal) and landowners assuming the cost and responsibility for maintaining offshoot ditches on their private *labores* (farmlands). In the first half of the nineteenth century, the average *labor* in the Río Pecos cultural basin cultivated by a single farmer was ten acres.

During the Mexican era, the military established presidios at Santa Fe, El Paso del Norte, San Fernando de Taos, and San Miguel del Vado. Since San Miguel was the port of entry for American merchants bound for Santa Fe, it became more important than the regional community of Las Vegas which did not attain official status until 1835.

Notwithstanding the intense attention given to political administration, the national government was incapable of providing adequate military protection for New Mexico's citizens. In actuality, the inhabitants of New Mexico, as best they could with inferior weapons, defended themselves against raids by Indian aggressors. Lacking training and equipment, the militia units in northern New Mexico stood helplessly as marauders committed atrocities in nearby *estancias, ranchos,* and villages. Whereas the muster roll for the veteran company at Santa Fe indicated 121 soldiers, the militia garrisoned at San Miguel del Vado numbered significantly fewer. In fact, all personnel of the presidial companies were required to procure their own horses, provisions, and weapons.

The national government's powerlessness to safeguard New Mexico was only one factor in a growing list of disaffection by the early 1840s. After two decades, the American-directed Santa Fe trade gradually displaced the Chihuahua merchants as brokers of the marketplace. Additionally, the gentle influx of Anglo American males into New Mexico, some of whom married women of old-line Hispanic families, softened the impact of an immigrant presence. As New Mexicans and Americans increased the pace of borrowing and sharing cultural traits, the traditional ties to Mexico weakened.

In political affairs two events attracted widespread attention in New Mexico. The first transpired in 1837, after Governor Albino Pérez, an inexperienced outsider, arrived in Santa Fe. His well-intentioned reforms in military organization and taxation provoked a rebellion in Chimayó which toppled his administration. Alarmed by the violence and destruction of property, the national government responded with the appointment of Manuel Armijo, a former executive and native of New Mexico. During Armijo's tenure in the governor's office the second threat to stability erupted.

The genesis of the threat originated in Texas in 1836 when Anglo American activists, aided by a number of native-born Tejanos, fomented a revolt against the centralist government of Antonio Lopez de Santa Anna. The wars of independence resulted in the creation of a Republic of Texas. Late in 1836 the congress of the Texas republic unilaterally defined the Rio Grande as the

PECOS—GATEWAY TO PUEBLOS & PLAINS

RÍO PECOS UNDER THE MEXICAN EAGLE

western boundary, northward from its mouth to its source and up to the forty-second parallel. This arbitrary legislation placed Santa Fe, New Mexico, east of the boundary and within the scope of the Texans' northern land claims.

A component in the grand design of Texas President Mirabeau B. Lamar was tapping the wealth of the Santa Fe trade and diverting the traffic southward through El Paso and then toward San Antonio, Austin, and Galveston. To implement his plan, Lamar appointed a military expedition of six companies, camouflaged as a trade commission, to invade New Mexico in the summer of 1841. The expedition's badly timed departure contributed to its disaster in the arid High Plains.

Anticipating aggression, Governor Armijo's alert militia captured the exhausted, ragged, starving Texans in September before they reached Santa Fe. Although Armijo dispatched the Texan prisoners to Mexico City for questioning and detention, the incident remained uppermost as a vivid memory in the consciousness of New Mexicans. Four years after the capture of the Texan–Santa Fe expedition, the United States annexed the republic as part of the westward movement.

The annexation of Texas quickly emerged as a burning issue between the governments of the United States and Mexico that led to a military conflict at Palo Alto on May 8, 1846. Shortly thereafter, New Mexico became occupied territory as the American army advanced toward Santa Fe, forcing Governor Armijo to retreat. The Río Pecos basin was the corridor through which General Stephen Watts Kearny's army entered New Mexico. At mid-afternoon of Tuesday, August 18, 1846, the general's soldiers hoisted the Stars and Stripes in the plaza of Santa Fe. Symbolically, an American eagle claimed a prominent space alongside the proud Mexican emblem.

Silver Mexican reales found their way to the United States as payment for the many new, imported American goods that came to Santa Fe.

PECOS
1821 · 1970

XIII WAYSTOP ON THE SANTA FE TRAIL
MARC SIMMONS

IN AN OPEN FIELD several hundred yards south of the old Pecos Mission a keen eye can find the scored ruts of spoked wheels left a century and a half ago by great freight wagons, nearing the end of their 800-mile journey from Missouri to Santa Fe. Those tracks, filled with new grass and flowers in spring, represent a small and fading monument to the stirring epic of the Santa Fe Trail.

That Pecos became closely linked in its own twilight years with the history of this historic roadway is a fact that can be explained by geography. The pueblo had been founded, long before the advent of Europeans, in the wide mouth of a natural funnel. Five miles or so west of the village, mesa walls constricted at Glorieta Pass to form the entrance of the long spout, a canyon leading down to Cañoncito in the direction of Santa Fe. Nowhere else in the vicinity could man on foot or horseback find such easy passage through the highlands. Spaniards from the Rio Grande Valley, beginning with Francisco Vásquez de Coronado in 1541, had used this route for centuries to gain access to the buffalo plains. Long afterward when Americans crossed the heartland of the continent to open trade with the New Mexican settlements, they could discover no better trail than the ancient one, winding alongside Pecos and over the summit of Glorieta Pass.

The history of the Santa Fe Trail begins in 1821 when William Becknell set forth from Franklin, Missouri, with several companions and a mule train of merchandise, intending to engage in commerce in the far Southwest. It was a landmark year, for Mexico had just won a hard-fought independence from Spain and was launching her experiment in nationhood. New Mexico, as a distant frontier province of Mexico, was delighted with the turn of events. Jealous Spain had kept her colonial borders tightly sealed, forbidding settlers like the New Mexicans from trading with American neighbors to the east. But independence brought a prompt dismantling of the barriers, with the result that Becknell found a generous welcome awaiting at Santa Fe and a ready market for his small stock of goods. His success, signaling the inauguration of overland trade between Mexico and the United States, led historians of a later date to bestow upon him the title, "Father of the Santa Fe Trail."

Although Becknell's sketchy account of his maiden

journey makes no mention of a stop at Pecos, it is certain that he paid the village at least a brief visit as it was on the route. However, another trader who passed by a few weeks later, Thomas James, took pains to describe the formidable pueblo he observed beside the trail. The Indians' houses, he thought, were "well built and showed marks of comfort and refinement." Yet, what impressed him most were the defensive measures taken by the inhabitants: the village resembled a walled fort with a gate leading into a large square. And he added, "on the roofs, which, like those of all the houses in Mexico, are flat, were large heaps of stone for annoying the enemy."

Thomas James slept in the "fort" that night, the first of many Americans who in the years following would take lodging in the pueblo. In 1846, less than a decade after the village's abandonment, young Susan Magoffin, bride of a veteran trader, paused with a merchant caravan at Pecos and recorded in her diary that her husband, "pointed out to me the door of a room in which he had once slept all night in some of his trips across the plains, and while some of the inhabitants still remained. It was the second story of a house which is now entirely fallen in."

Her remarks call attention to the two phases of Pecos's history associated with the trail. The first extended from 1821 down to 1838 when the handful of surviving Indians decided to give up their homes and move to Jemez Pueblo. The dwindling of Pecos, already far advanced when Becknell and James initially saw it, was the result of warfare, disease, and economic decline. Josiah Gregg, most celebrated chronicler of the Santa Fe Trail, described the mournful scene as he first witnessed it in the early 1830s.

> The traveller would often-times perceive but a solitary Indian, a woman or a child standing here and there like so many statues upon the roofs of their houses, with their eyes fixed on the eastern horizon, or leaning against a wall or fence, listlessly gazing at the passing stranger. At other times not a soul was to be seen in any direction, and the sepulchral silence of the place was only disturbed by the occasional barking of a dog or the cackling of hens.

His words convey the image of a ghost town in the making.

The first phase, in which travelers beheld an occupied pueblo and occasionally sought shelter under its roofs, gave way in 1838, with departure of the last residents, to the second phase, whereby Pecos became a somber relic of the trail and an object of curiosity, in short, a tourist attraction. At least one American wayfarer passed a night in the village soon after it was abandoned. In 1839 Matt Field found a ninety-year-old man with snow white hair living in the church and subsisting on a herd of goats he kept pastured nearby. He was a fugitive, Juan Cristobal Armijo, wanted by the authorities for killing a Mormon peddler. But he willingly shared his spare evening meal of porridge and goat's milk with Field, and, sitting at the foot of the ruined altar, recounted many of the folk legends that were already accumulating around the ghostly Pecos.

It was the funereal appearance of the decaying pueblo together with the bizarre stories about its early history, which quickly gained currency, that excited the wonder and imagination of Americans riding by on the Santa Fe Trail. Many of them had read William H. Prescott's *The Conquest of Mexico*, a book that filled the reader's head with stirring scenes involving Montezuma and the fall of the Aztecs. So, when travelers heard tales identifying Pecos as the birth place and original home of Montezuma, the ruined village took on a new aura of romance. Only a few of the less gullible expressed doubts about the Aztec connection, among them Susan Magoffin who pointedly wrote, "Tis probably a false tradition."

The Santa Fe traders were in the habit of camping with their freight wagons at a copious spring that issued from the left bank of the Pecos Arroyo about a half mile southeast of the village. After the evening meal, caravan members often strolled over to the ruins and took in the sights. Those who were keeping daily journals returned to the wagons and with quill and ink recorded by firelight their impressions of Pecos. It was usually their last night on the long trail because an early rising and a hard day's push brought the lumbering trains to Santa Fe by the following sunset.

About 1858 a Polish immigrant, recently mustered out of the army, settled on a flat next to the spring and started a ranch. Martin Kozlowski was actually a squatter, and he laid claim to a large block of surrounding land that included the remains of Pecos. Unhappily, he used the ancient mission church as a source of building materials, hauling away adobes and roof timbers to construct his own ranch house, barn and corrals. In time his home became a regular meal stop for the Barlow and Sanderson Company's Overland Stagecoaches. One passenger wrote that a substantial supper could be counted upon here, for Mrs. Kozlowski served fresh trout caught from the stream nearby.

By the coming of the railroad in 1880, which put the freight caravans and stagecoaches out of business, Pecos Pueblo had seen a great concourse of people flow by its walls. Initially, the traffic had been composed almost exclusively of Missouri merchants with their teamsters and stock drovers, men who pioneered the development of an international commerce between the United States and Mexico. That trade, while centering on Santa Fe, overflowed down the Chihuahua Trail and into the north Mexican provinces where Americans found an even larger market for their wares.

Bolts of fine cloth, shoes, hats and bonnets, religious articles, jewelry, mirrors, window glass, books, paper, assorted hardware, and even champagne and tinned oysters were among the items that figured prominently in the overland commerce. In exchange the traders received donkeys, mules, buffalo robes, velvet soft buckskins, Rio Grande blankets, and gold dust and nuggets from the Ortiz Mines south of Santa Fe. But most of all they carried home rawhide bags of Spanish silver "dollars" which the U.S. Congress as early as 1793 had authorized to circulate as legal coin. It is said that the influx of Spanish and Mexican silver prevented a run on the Bank of Missouri in 1839, and ultimately made that state's monetary affairs the soundest in the nation.

Then came a significant shift in 1846, the first year

WAYSTOP ON THE SANTA FE TRAIL

Mute testament to the once heavily-traveled Santa Fe Trail—scored ruts, now filled with grass and flowers, can be seen in the Pecos area.

of the Mexican War. General Stephen Watts Kearny's army of conquest marched up the Santa Fe Trail past Pecos Pueblo on its way to the seizing of Santa Fe and California. That event placed the western end of the trail in American hands and changed the character of the overland trade.

 In the years afterward, travelers who stopped to tour Pecos included 49ers bound for the California goldfields, soldiers posted to new forts established across the Southwest, government officials taking up duties in Santa Fe, and Catholic nuns assigned to schools recently built in the New Mexico Territory. Upon nearly all, the mysterious ruins of Pecos left a lasting impression. The pueblo stood at the gateway to the upper Río Grande Valley and to a land that was in almost every respect different from what the newcomers had left behind in the East.

 The Santa Fe Trail forms but a small chapter in the lengthy and memorable history of Pecos. Yet, it is an important part of that story, one that adds luster to the colorful saga of human achievement in the far Southwest.

XIV MANIFEST DESTINY PAUSES AT THE PECOS
K. JACK BAUER

TO MANY AMERICANS the colorful trading caravans passing along the Santa Fe Trail from Independence, Missouri to the New Mexico capital each spring represented proof of Manifest Destiny. They were visual evidence of the self-proclaimed superiority of the free and egalitarian society developed in the United States during the quarter century after the War of 1812. Whether or not the society was either free or egalitarian is debatable, but most Americans of the era believed so. Moreover, a large segment of the population accepted that it was the divine duty of the United States to extend the blessings of its system to those areas outside its borders which had suffered from the horrors of autocratic rule. For them it was the Manifest Destiny and duty of the United States to ensure, by force of arms if necessary, that the divinely inspired American socio-economic-political system be extended throughout the Americas. Some proponents argued that it should be imposed from Baffin Land in the north to Tierra del Fuego in the south.

Fundamental to the concept of Manifest Destiny was the notion that the United States should extend from the Atlantic to the Pacific oceans. One reality interfered. Much of the territory necessary to bring that about formed the lightly settled Mexican states of Nuevo Mexico and Alta California. James Knox Polk took office as President in 1845 with a plan to secure a Río Grande boundary and California for the United States. The Mexican government owed some $2 million to American creditors which it could not pay. Polk envisioned a solution under which the United States government would assume the debts in return for Mexico's acceptance of a Río Grande boundary and the transfer of title to California. Here the American president overlooked the reality of Mexican politics. No Mexican government which agreed to such an arrangement could hope to stay in office.

Polk's use of escalating pressure to convince Mexico that she must negotiate backfired. It created an ever stronger Mexican resistance to the surrender of national territory and led directly to the outbreak of fighting along the lower Río Grande in May 1846. The Polk administration adopted a strategy of limited military activity which was merely an extension of its prewar

By the time Kearny's army reached Pecos, the place was only a landmark, a curiosity stop along the trail. The Pecos and their history had passed into legend . . .

application of graduated pressure. It involved the occupation of California and key points such as Santa Fe in the northern Mexican states. Polk naively assumed that this would bring the Mexican government to the bargaining table.

New Mexico appeared to be an easy conquest. It was so sparsely settled that whoever held Santa Fe effectively controlled the state. Moreover, commercial ties to Old Mexico were so tenuous that New Mexico relied on the annual caravans from Missouri for most of its trade goods. Political connections with Mexico City were scarcely stronger. Governor Manuel Armijo ruled with little interference from his superiors and limited support from his fellow New Mexicans. Immediately upon the declaration of war against Mexico, Colonel Stephen Watts Kearny was ordered to prepare an expedition to seize New Mexico. Kearny, a fifty-two-year old frontier soldier, had entered service in 1812. After many years in the infantry he helped form and train the 1st Regiment of Dragoons. By 1846 he was one of the most experienced cavalry officers in the army, a brave and sensible field commander, who would prove to be an effective political administrator.

While Kearny's army gathered, two men set out from Independence for Santa Fe as heralds of the conquest. The first was a well-known Santa Fe trader George T. Howard. His assignment was to halt the caravans before they crossed into New Mexico. The second was another trader, James W. Magoffin, who rode on to Santa Fe where he claimed to have met with local leaders and undermined the defensive preparations.

Kearny's force, called the Army of the West, consisted of 1,458 men from the regular 1st Dragoons and a newly recruited regiment of Missouri mounted volunteers plus some field artillery. It left Fort Leavenworth in Kansas in late June for the 536-mile march to Bent's Fort on the Arkansas River. The trek across the hot, dusty, arid plains was an exercise in misery for the men and their horses. Yet they survived.

The Army of the West broke camp near Bent's Fort on August 2 for the 346-mile march to Santa Fe. The route generally followed that taken today by Interstate 25

U.S. Army tin cup ca. 1840. An indispensable part of every soldier's kit, its most important use was as a coffee pot—placed directly on the fire to boil each man's coffee.

through Raton Pass and on to Las Vegas and San Miguel. At Las Vegas Kearny, now wearing the stars of a Brigadier General, addressed about 150 inhabitants. He assured them that since Texas had claimed the area east of the Río Grande his men were there as protectors not invaders. He assured the Mexican citizens that the Americans would establish an effective and honest government which would protect their freedoms and respect their religion. In what were undoubtedly the most effective moves in easing the transition of power, he continued the local officials in their offices and paid for some corn which had been stolen by his troops.

Governor Armijo and his military commander, Colonel Manuel Pino, fortified Glorieta Pass and gathered there about 4,000 indifferently armed militia and volunteers. But Magoffin and other American agents had been at work undermining the will to resist. They argued that American occupation of Santa Fe was inevitable and would bring increased trade. They hinted that the western portions of the state would be left alone. As a result when Armijo called a council of war of his officers he found that they overwhelmingly opposed fighting. He thereupon disbanded the force and rode off to Chihuahua with his regular army bodyguard.

On August 17 Kearny's force bivouacked amid the luxuriant fields of grass at Pecos. As they became freed from camp routine some of the men inspected the remains of the old settlement, abandoned only seven years earlier. They gazed in wonder at the grandeur of the temple and retold the tale of the sacred fire. At Pecos the rotund Nicholas Quintaro rode into the American camp, dwarfing his little mule, and with a peal of laughter shouted the welcome news: "Armijo and his troops have gone to Hell and the cañon is all clear."

During the following morning the Army of the West marched through the Glorieta Pass with its silent cannon, each man undoubtedly saying a private prayer of thanks that it had not been defended, and entered Santa Fe. Acting Governor Juan Bautista Vigil y Alarid greeted them and watched as the Stars and Stripes ascended the flag pole at the governor's palace. A thirteen-gun salute echoed across the plaza to signal the transition of sovereignty.

During the next few days Kearny received the submissions of the chiefs of the nearby Indian pueblos and issued a proclamation annexing the state to the United States. That, like his later proclamation of a civilian government, was beyond his authority as the occupation commander or military governor. It was, however, a reasonable and sensible action. He did not have the officers necessary to operate a military government and was himself under orders to lead all men who could be spared to California. The Polk administration, as well as that of Zachary Taylor which followed it, upheld Kearny's actions and continued his temporary arrangement until 1850.

From Santa Fe detachments of Americans struck west to California and south to Chihuahua. Their campaigns, like the capture of Santa Fe, helped convince Mexican political leaders that the war must end. The Treaty of Guadalupe Hidalgo which brought peace in February 1848 transferred not only New Mexico and

MANIFEST DESTINY PAUSES AT THE PECOS

Arizona but also California, Nevada, and parts of Colorado and Utah to the United States. It solidified the American hold on the western coast of the continent and opened the transcontinental route to the Orient. Stephen Watts Kearny's little army had accomplished the key step in that expansion by establishing United States possession of the upper Río Grande valley and the area between it and California.

Acquisition of New Mexico thrust it into the vortex of the bubbling sectional controversy which swirled around slavery and the troublesome question of the location of the west Texas border. Texas's efforts to extend control over the area east of the Río Grande nearly led to an open conflict with the federal government, while the attempt to achieve statehood for the region opened the sores of sectionalism. As a result New Mexico had to accept territorial status in the Compromise of 1850 and wait until 1912 to become a state.

XV THE BATTLES OF GLORIETA PASS
BETSY SWANSON

It was Chance that armies of the North and South collided in the canyons of Glorieta Pass in March 1862. Yet, this ancient corridor between the Great Plains and the Río Grande seemed destined to serve as the battleground where the fate of the West was sealed early in the Civil War.

Through this rugged mountain pass, military supplies and troops, as well as emigrants and trade goods, had long been funneled on the Santa Fe Trail. Since 1861, the western boundary of the Confederate States of America had lain nearby at the New Mexico-Texas border. To extend that boundary to the Pacific Ocean was the Confederate plan, and the New Mexico Territory (which included the present state of Arizona) was the key to expansion.

Confederate possession of the Santa Fe Trail in northern New Mexico was essential, as was control over the proposed southern Pacific railroad route near the Mexican border. Uniting the Confederacy with transportation routes to the ports and goldfields of California would have bolstered both the economy and the chance for international recognition of the southern states. The Confederates also planned to annex part of Mexico. They envisioned this vast territorial expansion as extending their slave-based economy from sea to sea.

Initially, Confederate occupation of New Mexico had been successful. In July 1861, Colonel John R. Baylor and a force of Texans had easily occupied Fort Bliss near El Paso and Fort Fillmore near Las Cruces. Baylor had proclaimed the lower third of today's New Mexico and Arizona the Confederate Territory of Arizona and had named himself military governor. Panic-stricken but loyal Union garrisons had burned their posts and retreated to Fort Union in northeastern New Mexico to regroup under Colonel Edward Canby, federal commander of the Department of New Mexico.

Late in 1861, Confederate Brigadier General Henry Sibley had marched about 2,600 Texans to the lower Río Grande. The army, known as Sibley's Brigade, moved up the river in February 1862. Its gray-clad "Texas Rangers" were described as frontiersmen mounted on mustangs and armed with a rifle, tomahawk, bowie knife, pair of Colt revolvers, and lasso for throwing an enemy's horse.

Colonel Canby had meanwhile advanced with part of his force down the Río Grande to Fort Craig, below Socorro. On February 21, after a desperate battle on the

THE BATTLES OF GLORIETA PASS

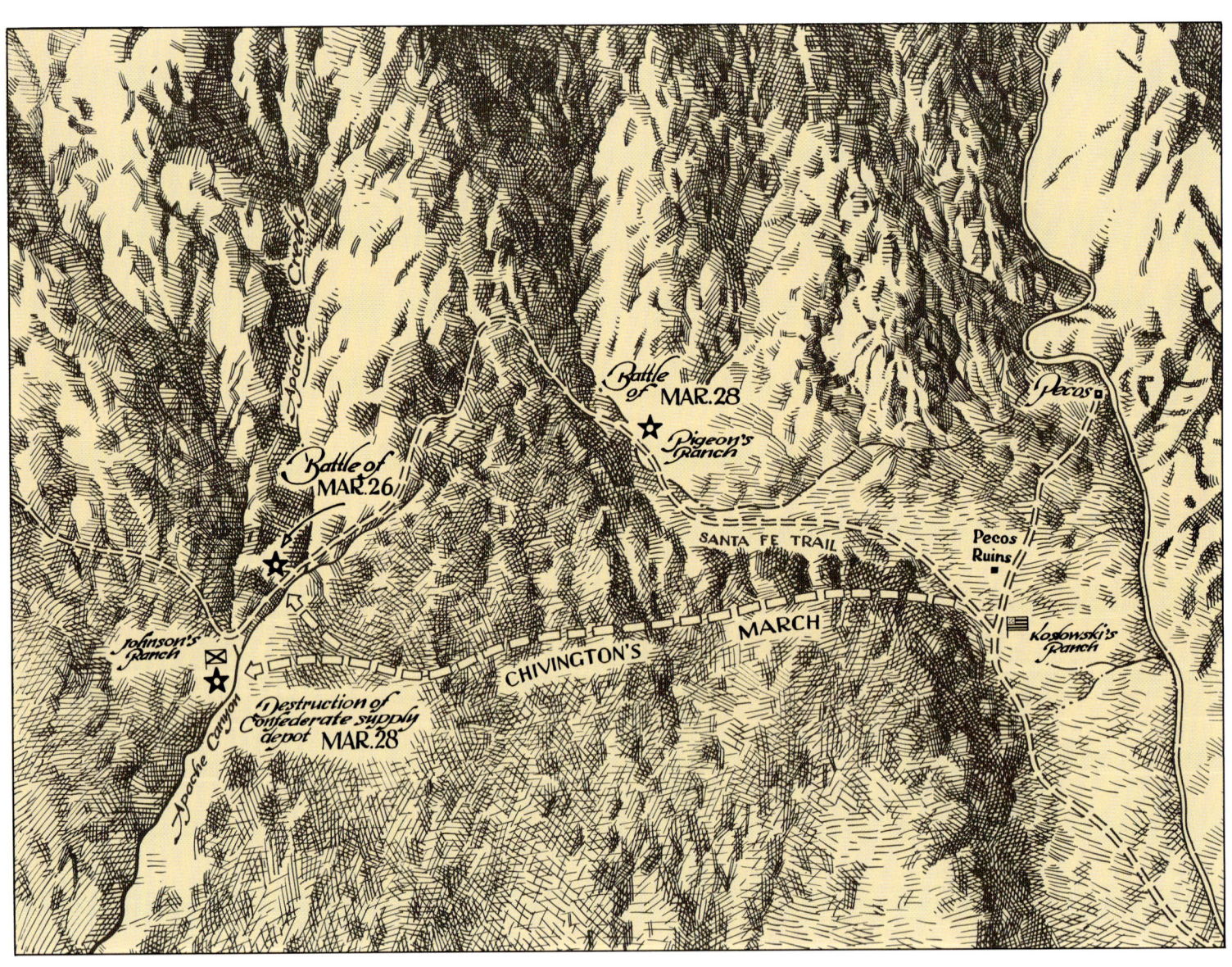

Río Grande at nearby Valverde, Union troops had reeled in defeat and retreated to Fort Craig. Sibley had then bypassed the fort to occupy Albuquerque on March 2 and Santa Fe on March 10.

While his men pillaged the capital, Sibley made plans to capture Fort Union, protector of the Santa Fe Trail. The fort lay eastward of Santa Fe, across the Sangre de Cristo Mountains, through Glorieta Pass. Sibley never engaged Fort Union, however, nor gained another success in New Mexico. His victories on the Río Grande marked the high point of the Confederacy in the West.

The fate awaiting the Texans at Glorieta Pass was that being met elsewhere in the trans-Mississippi campaigns, where the Confederates were beginning to suffer devastating reverses, crushing their dreams of expansion. They were being driven from parts of Missouri, Tennessee, and Kentucky. They were defeated at Pea Ridge, Arkansas, and at the slaughter of Shiloh. The closing-in of the Confederacy was to culminate a month later with the fall of New Orleans, the sealing of the Mississippi River, and the naval blockade of the Gulf Coast.

But Sibley's Rangers were flushed with victory as they advanced toward Glorieta Pass and Fort Union. General Sibley remained in Albuquerque, while Major Charles L. Pyron, in command of about 300 mounted men, advanced eastward from Santa Fe on the Santa Fe Trail. Lieutenant Colonel William R. Scurry, with several hundred Texans and an eighty-wagon supply train, moved forward from Albuquerque toward Galisteo, southeast of Santa Fe. They were to unite on the trail.

Pyron halted at the western end of Glorieta Pass, at a place called Cañoncito where the pass and trail were intersected by the canyons of Apache Creek and Río de las Indes. Here he camped in leisure at Johnson's Ranch and Stage Station. Since Colonel Canby had been left behind at Fort Craig, the Texans expected Fort Union to fall easily. They were unaware that Colorado troops had come to the defense of the fort and were camped at Bernal Springs, not many miles from the opposite end of the pass.

The First Colorado Volunteers, under Colonel John P. Slough, had left Denver for New Mexico in February, while Sibley's Brigade was moving up the Río Grande. Motivated largely by the restless desire of his Rocky Mountain miner volunteers to fight, Slough had left Fort Union with 1,342 men on March 22 to launch raiding operations. Besides Colorado troops, the force included regular U.S. Army cavalry, infantry and artillery units, and several companies of New Mexico Volunteers.

While camped at Bernal Springs, Slough sent an advance raiding party of 418 men toward Santa Fe. It was led by Major John M. Chivington, a former missionary and Methodist Church elder, called by his men "the fighting parson." Late on the night of March 25 they reached Kozlowski's Ranch and Stage Stop, near the ruins of the Pecos Indian Pueblo and Mission Church, where they camped at a spring.

On the morning of March 26, Chivington advanced westward through the pass. He reached the summit of the divide in the early afternoon. On the descending slope he surprised the Confederates moving eastward up the

Santa Fe Trail near the intersection of steep-walled Apache Cañon. The Colorado Volunteers, Army Regulars, and New Mexico Volunteers rushed toward the Texans. Though taken off guard, Major Pyron ordered the formation of a skirmish line. Chivington employed enveloping tactics by sending companies of riflemen up the mountain sides to shoot down upon the enemy's line. Pyron then ordered his men to pull back, ending what was officially called the First Skirmish of Apache Cañon.

The Confederates established a new defense line farther down the trail, where the canyon abruptly curved around a steep rocky bluff. They made the precipice their "fortress" and destroyed a bridge below it over which the trail crossed a deep arroyo. In the road they planted their howitzers and their red flag emblazoned with the "Lone Star" of Texas. Chivington employed the same enveloping tactics, and hand-to-hand fighting ensued among the rocks and scrub trees. The shouts of the men, roar of cannon, rattle of small arms, clash of metal, blare of bugles, and crash of falling rocks resounded against the canyon walls.

After an hour of fighting, Pyron ordered withdrawal when Union skirmishers began to flank his artillery. As the Texans retreated, the Union cavalry reserve charged headlong through the canyon. Finding the bridge at the arroyo torn up, the horsemen leapt the sixteen-foot span and galloped into the midst of the retreating enemy. Only one horse failed to make the jump and fell with its rider into the gulch. The Texans were routed, captured, wounded, or killed. It was their first defeat in New Mexico.

Sundown had come and darkness fell quickly in the casualty-strewn canyon. Chivington abandoned pursuit and brought an end to the Battle of Apache Cañon. He withdrew his troops to Pigeon's Ranch, a stage stop in the eastern part of the pass, where he established a hospital for the wounded of both sides. Pyron retreated to Johnson's Ranch and sent a courier to Scurry requesting reinforcement. Chivington sent notice to Slough for assistance and fell back the next day to Kozlowski's Ranch where water was more plentiful.

After a night march over snow-covered mountains, Scurry arrived at Johnson's Ranch at 3 a.m. on March 27. Slough reached the Union camp at Kozlowski's at 2 a.m. that same morning. Both armies hesitated at opposite ends of the pass, then, on the morning of March 28, both simultaneously advanced. They came together at Pigeon's Ranch. The encounter there, called the Battle of Glorieta, was the decisive Civil War engagement in the West.

The Union advance was in two columns. The main force of about 700 men marched on the trail under Slough. Chivington, with about 450 men, took a diverging path over the top of Glorieta Mesa, on the south side of the pass, to attack the enemy's rear. They were guided by Lieutenant Colonel Manuel Chavez, of the Second New Mexico Volunteers, and civilian James Collins. The effective force of the Confederate advance also numbered about 700, under Scurry's command.

At mid-morning, as the Union troops were resting at Pigeon's Ranch and filling their canteens at the well, Rebel grapeshot and shell came crashing down upon them. The Yankees rushed forward with their artillery to attack the Confederate line about a half-mile ahead among the trees, hills, and arroyos. But throughout the seven-hour battle that followed, the Union force remained in positions of defensive retreat. For a time, the Union troops held a strong position behind the adobe walls of the ranch, with riflemen on a high rock ledge to the north of the house, and artillery in the road and on a mesa to the south. The roar of cannon reverberated from the mountain sides "like a heavy and continuous drumming of a military band." With savage courage, the Texans charged five times across an open meadow into the very mouths of the cannon, and climbed the rock ledge to drive the Federals back down the road.

    The Confederate victory was turned into defeat when Scurry received word that his supply train, containing his army's ammunition, food, and blankets, had been destroyed by Chivington's rear attack at Johnson's Ranch. Having crossed Glorieta Mesa, the Union detachment climbed down a sheer rock cliff overlooking the wagons, routed, captured, or killed the guards, burned the wagons, killed the horses and mules, and climbed back up the mesa to rejoin the Union camp that night. This strategic action resulted in Confederate retreat from New Mexico, during which many died from hunger, thirst, or Indian attack. Only one-third of Sibley's army returned safely to Texas. The Battle of Glorieta, often called "the Gettysburg of the West," thus forced the Confederacy to abandon its plans of conquest in the West.

Cannonball found on the Glorieta Battlefield. "We charged up a hill . . . towards an enemy who were hidden and invisible and who waited patiently for us to approach to shoot us down." Rebels on the Rio Grande: The Civil War Journal of A.B. Peticolas.

XVI THE SANTA FE RAILWAY
VERNON J. GLOVER & JOHN McCALL

THE COMING OF SURVEYORS

for the railroad to New Mexico in the 1850s was an event of such import that it can only be compared to the appearance of *conquistadores* over three centuries before. The glittering brass transits and one-hundred-foot steel "chains" in the hands of determined civil engineers were instruments of empire as surely as were the muskets and lances of the earlier invaders. Ancient trails, which still pass the abandoned pueblo of Pecos, attracted railroaders for the same reasons that earlier travelers were enticed to follow them as the easiest and best routes around the southern end of the Rocky Mountains.

By the mid-1870s three railroads were extending track toward New Mexico. The Atchison, Topeka and Santa Fe (AT&SF) had begun building from Topeka, Kansas, in 1869 and by 1876 its tracks had reached Pueblo, Colorado, where the company suspended efforts long enough to recoup financially and consider the possible routes across the Rocky Mountains. The narrow gauge Denver & Río Grande (D&RG) had built south from Denver and had extended branches south to El Moro, Colorado, and west into La Veta Pass. And the powerful Southern Pacific, backed by Collis P. Huntington, was building eastward from Los Angeles along a route close to the Mexican border. None of the companies was in a position to quickly build through New Mexico, but they watched each other carefully.

The developing storm broke during early 1878 when the Southern Pacific interests made an overt attempt to use the Territorial Legislature to pass an act intended to exclude other railroads from the territory. Caught by surprise, the AT&SF and D&RG responded with accelerated campaigns of construction into New Mexico. The AT&SF construction company, incidentally, carried the name New Mexico & Southern Pacific RR, one that has intrigued and confused historians ever since.

In early February 1878, hastily recruited construction crews of the D&RG and the AT&SF met head on in a nighttime confrontation at Raton Pass. The AT&SF won the ground, thereby setting its route into New Mexico. But the future path of the D&RG was to be forever turned west.

The AT&SF quickly learned about mountain

railroading as it built and operated its line over Raton Pass and down into New Mexico. A notable achievement was the operation of the famous "Uncle Dick," then the world's largest locomotive at a weight of fifty-eight tons. The railroad reached Las Vegas, New Mexico, on July 4, 1879, where it paused briefly to gather its forces and to determine its route across New Mexico.

Throughout the summer of 1879 the NM&SP purchased and accumulated construction materials at Las Vegas. Great stacks of cross ties, iron rails, and bridge timbers piled up in the construction yard while the chief engineer was determining the best route to use toward the Río Grande. The most economical route would strike out directly across the High Plains toward the southwest. It would bridge the Pecos River near Villanueva and then enter the Río Grande Valley through Abo Canyon at the southern end of the Manzano Mountains.

The second route envisioned would have run north of the first, crossing the plains via Canyon Blanco and Tijeras Canyon west to Albuquerque. Since this route offered no substantial advantages over the first and was more expensive to build, it was never given serious consideration.

The third route contemplated would have followed old trails around the southern end of the Rockies, via Glorieta Pass, and have reached the Río Grande at Santo Domingo. It would have been the most expensive of the three to construct and operate, but it possessed a number of local advantages. First, the Glorieta route afforded easy access to the timber stands along the upper Pecos River which would allow the railroad to cut cross ties from nearby forests and save the costs of purchasing them. Second, the line would pass near the numerous promising mines of the southern Rockies. This route would also provide the closest access to the ancient and territorial capital of Santa Fe, though, interestingly, the railroad's engineering studies concluded that business from Santa Fe would accrue to the railroad even if it did not enter the town itself.

Farther down the line, at Galisteo Creek, the route passed close to the coal and mineral deposits below Galisteo before it served all the pueblos and villages along the Río Grande. Overall, the Glorieta route threading its way among hills and mesas was relatively protected from winds and drifting snows, and it offered terminal sites in favorable locations with good water.

Exhaustive studies dictated the choice of the Glorieta route, and the construction of the NM&SP was resumed during the summer of 1879. Before long the entire route was a beehive of activity as hundreds of horse-drawn scrapers shaped the roadbed, cutters dragged hewn cross ties down from the surrounding mountains, and bridge carpenters erected dozens of trestles across streams and over gullies. Track layers and supply trains followed as the railroad took shape.

The railroad, having learned an expensive lesson on Raton Pass, kept its grades as low as possible as the line passed through Kearny's Gap, crossed the valley of Tecolote Creek, and dropped down to the Pecos River crossing near Ribera. This need to lessen the grade resulted in the famous S-curve at Ribera, where the terrain dropped away more steeply than the railroad desired. The sweeping curves added the necessary length to ease the grade.

From the Pecos crossing to Glorieta Summit, the track climbed a long, heavy grade of 1.70 percent, broken only by a short stretch near Rowe. The line followed the northeast face of Glorieta Mesa in sight of the ruins of the Pecos Mission and Pueblo. The track at Glorieta crossed the summit in a deep cut.

On the west side of the pass, the track followed Galisteo Creek down a very steep 3 percent grade through the tortuous confines of Apache Canyon. It was exactly ten miles down to Galisteo Junction (soon to be renamed Lamy) where the grade eased to 1.42 percent or less for the remaining descent to the Río Grande Valley.

The railroad, completed to Lamy by February 9, 1880, was a difficult road to operate—and it remains so today. In the early years there were numerous runaways, especially on the steeper west side. Washouts were a regular spring and summer hazard, and numerous derailments were blamed on rain-softened roadbeds. The AT&SF met the challenge with new air brakes on its trains and a fleet of fifty-ton Baldwin locomotives, the direct descendants of "Uncle Dick." Vulnerable timber trestles were replaced with iron spans on masonry abutments, and stone ballast from mountain quarries firmed up the track. Within a few years, the Santa Fe Trail had been transformed into an increasingly busy transcontinental railroad.

The early decision to bypass the capital of Santa Fe was justified when in 1879 the citizens of Santa Fe County voted to issue bonds to pay for the construction of an eighteen-mile branch railroad from Lamy to Santa Fe. This line was opened for traffic on February 16, 1880, and, for a few months thereafter it was served by passenger trains from Kansas City. Train service of one class or another has continued to this day.

Most of the other projections implicit in the early engineering studies of the Glorieta route came to pass. Lumbering became a big industry for a few years, and nearly thirty sawmills were operating in the southern Sangre de Cristo Mountains by 1882, causing the AT&SF to station a "pick-up locomotive" at Baughl's Station, near Rowe, to collect carloads of timber. Prospecting boomed in the mountains, although few mines achieved steady production. The Evangeline mine on the Pecos River, rich in copper laced with gold and silver, failed because its ores were unsuited to the smelting techniques of the era. The new mining camp at Cerrillos prospered, first due to the metal mines and later with the coal mines at Rogers and Madrid.

The effect of the railroad on New Mexico was dramatic. An old way of life changed overnight, and New Mexico truly became part of the United States. Across the territory, hundreds of cars of coal were shipped daily. The number of cattle increased from 347,000 in 1880 to 1,630,000 in 1890. Innumerable towns were created and grew along the railroad tracks. The number of banks grew from only two before the railroad to over fifty, signaling the end of the mercantile capitalism of the Santa Fe Trail days.

By 1900 the railroad through Glorieta had become a busy portion of a revitalized AT&SF system, following its

Pecos Ruins, a tourist stop promoted by the Atchison, Topeka and Santa Fe Railroad Indian Detour bulletin of February, 1927.

1893 receivership. Trains were longer, and they were routinely headed by two locomotives, an expensive operation. The California trade resulted in many fast trains over the line carrying passengers, mail, fruit, and vegetables. But the next few years were to see many changes take place.

The economics of running trains over the steep passes at Raton and Glorieta caused AT&SF management to consider an entirely new main line—this one running from central Kansas via Amarillo and Abo Canyon to a junction with the old main line just west of Belen, New Mexico. Opened for traffic in July 1908, the Belen Cut-off immediately siphoned off the heaviest and fastest of the through freight trains, though the railroad past Pecos continued to carry a large number of trains as traffic continued to increase overall.

The rapid introduction of steel-framed cars during this period had a profound impact on the railroad itself. Within a very few years, a new railroad was built in place of the original one. New locomotives, ten-drivered and weighing 150 tons, pulled long strings of steel cars on new rail over new steel bridges. Speed increased and so did efficiency. Fewer crews were needed, and towns such as Raton and Las Vegas ceased to grow.

Nevertheless, a lot of freight traffic continued to roll over Glorieta Summit. Much of it was coal from the north and overflow traffic from the Belen Cut-off. The old Evangeline mine finally came to life as the Pecos mine of the American Metal Company. From 1927 to 1939, the mine and its mill shipped out by rail thousands of tons of concentrates rich in zinc, lead, copper, gold, and silver. As recently as 1966 to 1983 a weekly unit-train carried 10,000 tons of coal every trip from York Canyon in northern New Mexico to California steel mills by way of Glorieta.

More and more people traveled to California, and most of the passenger trains were routed through Glorieta. To serve them and the ever-growing New Mexico tourist trade, a string of Fred Harvey railroad station hotels was opened along the tracks. From a relatively unsuccessful beginning with the Montezuma above Las Vegas came The Cardenas (Trinidad), The Castañeda (Las Vegas), El Ortiz (Lamy), The Alvarado (Albuquerque), and El Navajo (Gallup). The finest of them all was La Fonda at Santa Fe.

There were times when the California Limited ran in no fewer than seven solid Pullman sections, each having its luxurious Fred Harvey dining car and its elegant observation lounge on the tail end. Beginning in 1926, many tourists saw New Mexico under the guidance of Indian Detours, a company which provided guided tours of the state in big automobiles and buses. The Pecos ruins were among their earliest stopping places.

Over the years many trains unmatched for style, luxury, and speed have passed by Pecos. The California Limited was supplanted by the Chief, which, in turn, was replaced by the Super Chief. Glistening stainless-steel streamliners took over the runs, headed by red and yellow diesel-electric locomotives. The coach passengers on El Capitan were treated to the finest rolling stock of all in the double-deck "hi-level" trains of 1956. The contemporary Amtrak train which passes Pecos and Glorieta is outfitted with near duplicates in its Superliner cars.

Further changes to the railroad may be guaranteed by the possible merger of the two old enemies—the Atchison, Topeka & Santa Fe and the Southern Pacific—into a western super-railroad to be known as the Southern Pacific & Santa Fe. Plans for new routes, new traffic patterns, and the role of the old main line are by no means clear cut at this time. One thing is certain, however. Nothing in the future can alter the rich heritage and important historical role which has been played by the Atchison, Topeka and Santa Fe's old main line which passes so near to Pecos National Monument.

XVII A. V. KIDDER & PECOS
RICHARD B. WOODBURY

IN 1910, A.V. KIDDER first saw the ruins of Pecos Pueblo in 1910, taken there by his friend Kenneth M. Chapman, a Santa Fe artist and illustrator who was soon to become an authority on modern Pueblo pottery. Five years later Kidder unhesitatingly chose Pecos when the opportunity came for a major archeological program under his direction.

As an undergraduate at Harvard, however, Kidder was headed for a medical career. But he found the required courses, such as chemistry, far less attractive than the anthropology "electives" he happened upon. And in 1907 he had the lucky accident of learning that three student volunteers were wanted for an archeological expedition in the Southwest. He was accepted, spent the summer in the Four Corners country, on the Pajarito Plateau, at Mesa Verde, and in Santa Fe, and fell in love with the Southwest and with archeology. In the winter of 1908-1909, following his graduation, he traveled with his parents in Greece and Egypt, and there saw the large-scale, multi-year pattern of Old World archeology. On his entry into graduate study he sought out the courses of the renowned Egyptologist G. A. Reisner, whose techniques of excavation, record keeping, and analysis were far ahead of his time. These greatly impressed Kidder and he later applied them and improved on them.

In 1914 Kidder received his Ph.D. from Harvard in archeology with a thesis entitled "Southwestern Ceramics: Their Value in Reconstructing the History of the Ancient Cliff Dwelling and Pueblo Tribes: An Exposition from the Point of View of Type Distinctions." It formally presented the ideas that Kidder had been developing on classifying pottery as precisely and completely as ornithologists classified birds (he had been a bird-watcher from his early years) and then making comparisons from level to level within a site and between one site and another. In this way both time sequences and regional relationships and differences could be determined. This approach has been commonplace in archeology for so long now that it is hard to realize how important and revolutionary it was at the time. Kidder was the first archeologist with southwestern interests to receive a Ph.D. in the United States.

In the summer of 1914 Kidder was back in the field with Samuel J. Guernsey, excavating in the Kayenta area of northern Arizona for Harvard's Peabody Museum.

Pecos Pueblo, just fifty years after abandonment, before drifting soils and encroaching vegetation hid the rock walls.

They demonstrated by stratigraphic evidence that "Basketmaker" remains were older than "Pueblo" remains, previously only a speculation. Also, their report, published in 1919, gave the clearest definitions yet written of the two distinct but related cultural patterns, and laid the groundwork for much of the next thirty years' research in southwestern archeology.

When Phillips Academy, in Andover, Massachusetts, decided to support a large-scale, long-term program in archeology, Kidder was asked to plan and direct it. The choice was ideally appropriate, as he was already highly regarded for his vigorous development of new archeological methods and ideas, oriented to problems rather than museum specimens, and based on systematic, detailed collection and analysis of information.

Kidder immediately chose Pecos as the site for Phillips Academy's program. As he wrote later, Pecos had impressed him in 1910 with the great variety of potsherds seen on the surface, "all the varieties then known in the Río Grande, from the ancient black-on-white to the obviously modern." Here, then, was a ruin of long duration, with its final occupation well within historic times (the last inhabitants of Pecos left in 1838). Kidder felt that the sequence of pottery types that he could work out there would prove a basis for giving relative dates to the hundreds of other ruins in the Río Grande area. At the age of thirty Kidder was ready to set an example of archeological field work and reporting that was to be a continuing inspiration to his contemporaries and successors.

Kidder began work at Pecos in 1915, and for twelve

Utility ware found with a Pecos burial. The maker of this fire-blackened vessel shaped the handles in the form of animals.

years (except for two years of World War I service and one year of nonarcheological research related to Pecos) he spent long summers, excavating at Pecos or nearby older sites. He was accompanied in the field work by his wife, Madeleine, who not only washed, sorted, and classified countless thousands of potsherds, but also oversaw camp arrangements. Kidder's approach was two-fold. One part involved digging long, deep trenches that began outside the ruins and the surrounding trash dumps, working inward, cross sectioning the layers of rubbish, and further in within the ruins, showing the sequence of building and rebuilding of the pueblo. The second part consisted of clearing rooms within the pueblo to examine building techniques, furnishings (fireplaces, benches, etc.), and to define the size and shapes of the various blocks of rooms on the mesa. From the refuse the rooms contained, and the occasional broken pots on the floor under a collapsed roof, he could assign the rooms' relative dates and work out the long history of the town. This first year he had the assistance of Jesse L. Nusbaum, who repaired the Spanish mission church, which had been subjected to vandalism for nearly a century. This required extensive and careful digging to expose and then strengthen the foundations.

Kidder could interpret the successive strata in his trenches and the refuse in abandoned rooms because during the first summer he worked out the eight main types of Pecos pottery, and determined their chronological sequence. This work also confirmed the value of the stratigraphic technique that Nels C. Nelson of the American Museum of Natural History had just introduced to the Southwest in his work in the Galisteo Basin twenty miles to the west. This series of eight Pecos pottery types became the cornerstone for deciphering the complex history of Pecos and its changes, growth, decline, and abandonment.

The next year the trenching was expanded to the north and west sides of the mesa, and the North Terrace area was investigated in detail. It proved to be the oldest part of the ruin, with only black-on-white pottery, its beginning placed at about A.D. 1300. Here, as in the trenches in the rubbish heaps, hundreds of burials were found, some in the refuse of abandoned rooms, some under floors. By 1926 over 1,800 skeletons in various states of completeness and preservation had been excavated at Pecos and nearby sites. They formed the basis of the landmark study, *Indians of Pecos*, by E. A. Hooton of Harvard, which examined the relation of the Pecos people to other Indian groups, reconstructed the growth and decline of the town's population, identified some of their diseases, and calculated their life expectancies.

One of the major results of Kidder's work at Pecos was publication in 1924 of his *Introduction to the Study of Southwestern Archaeology*, a summary of all that was then known on the subject and the first synthesis of the archeology of any New World region. Gordon Willey of Harvard University later wrote that "It is a rarity in that it introduced systematics to a field previously unsystematized, and, at the same time, it is vitally alive and unpedantic . . . Kidder put the classification of potsherds into southwestern archeology without removing or obscuring the people who made the pottery." It quickly became and still remains a classic of archeological writing.

In addition to bringing order out of chaos in the study of pottery and demonstrating the value of stratigraphic excavation, Kidder's work at Pecos was the first thoroughly planned, multiseason work in New Mexico; it showed how much more could be learned this way than by "hit-and-run" archeology, a few weeks here, a few there, and next summer at yet another tempting ruin. He also pioneered the use of related studies to illuminate archeological problems, such as the technical analysis of pottery clays, pigments, and tempering by Anna O. Shepard, the ethnographic study of San Ildefonso pottery making by Carl E. Guthe, both of which aided in understanding Pecos pottery, and the study of Jemez Pueblo, to which the Pecos survivors went in 1838, by Elsie Clews Parsons. Kidder's work at Pecos is also notable for the series of reports he published, beginning with the 1924 volume already mentioned (which includes summaries of each season's field work through 1922) and ending with the eighth volume in the series in 1958, a 380-page masterpiece of archeological reporting and interpretation modestly called *Pecos, New Mexico: Archaeological Notes*.

Kidder's leadership in southwestern archeology is nowhere reflected more clearly than in an event in the summer of 1927. During the preceding winter he conceived the idea of inviting all active southwestern archeologists to meet at his field camp in August, "in order," as he wrote to his good friend Earl H. Morris, "to thrash out at leisure the various questions of problems, method, and nomenclature." For three days some forty-five archeologists met morning and afternoon, sitting on the ground under the junipers and discussing a wide range of topics. One foremost on their minds was the prospect that tree-ring dating, developed by astronomer A. E. Douglass, would soon be complete from modern trees back to the timbers and charcoal of prehistoric ruins (as indeed it was the next year); they discussed problems of standardizing names for pottery shapes and decorative motifs, and for architecture. Each field worker described informally his recent work. But by far the most important discussion centered on the comprehensive chronological system which Kidder is generally credited with devising, specifying criteria (mostly ceramic and architectural details) for three successive Basketmaker time periods and five Pueblo periods. It ran from the earliest known southwestern materials up to historic times. During the next decades the "Pecos Classification," as it was promptly named, underwent refinements but no basic changes except for the realization that it applied only to the area now called Anasazi.

But not only did the Pecos Classification make a lasting contribution to southwestern archeology, the conference itself became an important continuing event. It quickly became a major means by which field workers could communicate their findings to each other, try out new ideas, and keep abreast of the increasingly large and varied work being done in the entire Southwest. Attendance has grown enormously but the format has changed little—informal reports on recent field work,

A. V. Kidder, lower right, and his friend Rachael Lothrop, left, survey the extensive trenches dug in the North Pueblo midden, 1915.

discussion of important current problems, sometimes a symposium on a topic of broad interest, and always a high degree of informality. There are no memberships, no dues, no permanent officers, no headquarters, and no regularly published reports. There is only a mailing list made up from each conference's participants and a modest registration fee each year. Its influence has been enormous, as virtually every field worker in the Southwest has attended at one time or another, often for many years without a break. New information is immediately available, ideas can be circulated, argued, and modified. Kidder's leadership continued for many years, and long after his death in 1963 the purposes he outlined in 1927 have continued little changed:

> to bring about contact between workers in the Southwestern field; to discuss fundamental problems of Southwestern History [in which he included prehistory], and to formulate plans for coordinated attack upon them; to pool knowledge of facts and techniques; and to lay the foundations for unified systems of nomenclature.

Kidder sometimes said that he would have published more, and soon, on Pecos and his southwestern research if he had not begun a second career in 1929, taking charge of the extensive and long continuing Maya archeological program of the Carnegie Institution of Washington. This program, by coincidence, was begun in 1915 by Sylvanus G. Morley, who, with Kidder, had been a student volunteer on the 1907 trip to the Southwest to work with Edgar L. Hewett. For the Maya program Kidder worked in Yucatan and Guatemala each winter and returned nearly every summer to the Southwest, visiting the field work areas of his many friends and colleagues. And each August he brought his knowledge and perspective to the Pecos Conference, as it came to be known officially. His career as a Maya archeologist was as distinguished as his southwestern career. But his name remains particularly linked at Pecos, where he made unique and significant contributions, justifying his faith that a long program and a multifaceted research approach (which he later applied in Maya archeology) would produce unparalleled results in understanding the past of Native Americans.

The first Pecos Conference, August 1927. Front, left to right: Mrs. Oliver Ricketson (Edith B), Mrs. Sylvanus C. Morley (Frances), Charles Amsden, Earl H. Morris, Ann A. Morris, Dr. A. L. Kroeber, Miss Charlotte Gower, Dr. J. A. B. Scherer, Mrs. C. B. Cosgrove (Harriet); Standing, left to right: Oliver Ricketson, Dr. J. B. Thoburn, Dr. E. B. Renaud, Jesse L. Nusbaum, Dr. A. E. Douglass, Harry H. Shapiro, Neil M. Judd, Robert Wauchope, Kenneth Chapman, Mrs. A. V. Kidder (Madeline), Dr. A. V. Kidder, Mrs. Frank H. H. Roberts, Jr., Frank H. H. Roberts, Miss Clara Lee Frapps (Tanner), Lansing Bloom, Mrs. Hulda Penner (Mrs. Emil Haury), Emil W. Haury, Dean Byron Cummings, Dr. Walter Hough, M. R. Harrington, Leslie Spier. Photo taken by C. B. Cosgrove.

XVIII COLONIAL PERIOD ARCHEOLOGY AT PECOS
ALDEN C. HAYES

THE NATIONAL PARK SERVICE

acquired what had been New Mexico's Pecos State Monument in 1965, inheriting responsibility for the protection of the ancient ruins. The great North Pueblo was in good condition. Its excavator, A. V. Kidder, had followed the practice of backfilling an excavated room with the spoil from the room next to it so that the Indians' masonry walls were protected from the elements. This was not the case at the Spanish mission structures. The exposed walls of the adobe church and the attached convento were less weatherproof and had long been further deteriorated by timber pillagers, treasure-seekers, and from sightseers. A project was planned that would excavate, stabilize, and prepare the church and convento for exhibit. Jean McQuirt Pinkley was selected for the job, and she started work the first of July 1966, after twenty years experience in planning and managing a program of ruins stabilization and interpretation at Mesa Verde National Park.

Pinkley's was not the first trowel, however, to prod the old, historic buildings. In 1915, Edgar L. Hewett, Director of the Museum of New Mexico, received an application from Alfred Kidder, an old student of his Pajarito Plateau field school for archeologists, for permission to start excavations in Pecos Pueblo for Phillips Academy. Hewett readily issued the permit and recruited another ex-student, Jesse Nusbaum, to clean up debris from the church and to stabilize its crumbling walls while Kidder's crew dug in the pueblo. Nusbaum had earlier experience in shoring up old walls at Mesa Verde, and having worked with Kidder before, was eager to accept. The salary of $150 a month, unusually generous for the day, probably was no small consideration. Nusbaum left his job helping Fred Harvey set up the "Indian Room" at the Alvarado Hotel in Albuquerque, and rode his motorcycle out to Pecos. With laborers from San Antonio de Pecos he excavated the nave of the church, going below the floor to pour concrete curbings at the base of the walls. In the process he removed many burials which were reburied when the floor was backfilled.

Ten years later, in 1925, Kidder was still at it. That summer he detailed Susan Valliant to trench the area in

Without a roof, the exposed adobe walls of Pecos church and convento were slowly succumbing to the elements. This photograph of Adolph Bandelier at Pecos was taken in 1880, thirty-five years before Jesse L. Nusbaum began stabilization.

front of the church for more burials to be used in E. A. Hooton's study of the skeletons, supplementing the collection of human remains from the trash mounds of the pueblo. In a deep cut nearly fifty feet west of the facade of the church, Valliant ran into a massive stone wall well below the present surface. There was neither time nor money to investigate further, and having the bones she needed, she refilled her trench.

Adobe will last nearly forever if protected from the elements, but without a roof the open shell of the Pecos church in 1938, twenty-three years after Nusbaum's attention, was again showing signs of melting into the mesilla. Hewett was able to get money from the state and free labor from the federal Civilian Conservation Corps for work at Pecos. He brought in Edwin N. Ferdon, a Museum of New Mexico archeologist who had been excavating—stabilizing as he went—at the mission of Nuestra Señora de la Concepción at Quarai. Soon after the project was underway Ferdon was relieved by William Boris Witkind, fresh out of the University of New Mexico, who reported to work on a bitter day in January 1939. Hewett's men were not summertime archeologists—they worked year round.

Witkind met difficult conditions. With an unskilled crew that varied in numbers from day to day depending on what other work the Forest Service had for the men, and with no one to help with technical, administrative, or supervisory duties, he rebuilt the wall that connected the church to the pueblo. He also cleaned the floor of the church, removed some of Nusbaum's concrete abutments and restabilized the wall footings with less obtrusive

Jesse L. Nusbaum's crew stabilizing and reinforcing the south transept wall of the Pecos mission church, ca. 1915.

work, and excavated the cloisters and adjacent rooms of the convento. In probing for the bases of the walls of the church's south sacristy, Witkind also found deeply buried sections of stone masonry. Their complete exposure was not part of the job so, like Valliant, he noted their presence and covered them up. Witkind got some relief from a strenuous schedule in the summer of 1939 when he was joined by John M. Corbett (later to become the Chief Archeologist of the National Park Service) who helped supervise the crew and excavate much of the South Pueblo.

Without the work done by Nusbaum and Witkind, Jean Pinkley might have found little of the church left to put on exhibit, but an undisturbed ruin is easier to work with than one which has been dug and refilled. She spent much of the summer of 1966 finding out where her predecessors had dug and where they had not. Despite a slow, groping start, Pinkley and her crew had excavated or reexcavated two-thirds of the convento before the first snowfall, including the discovery of a white-plastered cellar in an open compound next to what was probably the kitchen.

In the spring of 1967 Pinkley turned her attention to the church. Like earlier diggers, she was concerned with problems of preserving the old adobe walls, but unlike Valliant and Witkind she had time literally to get to the bottom of the structure to learn its story; and she was determined to do so. In the process she, too, struck the thick, buried masonry footings. Her Hispanic crew from the village of Pecos shared with her the excitement of tracing the outlines of the foundations of an older and much larger buttressed church. The discovery was an important breakthrough.

The 1945 translation of an account by Fray Alonso de Benavides of New Mexico written between 1625 and 1629 revealed a discrepancy. Benavides described the church at Pecos as ". . . of peculiar construction and beauty, very spacious, with room for all the people of the pueblo." The ruin we all knew was quite ordinary as New Mexico missions go and hardly large enough to accommodate half of the pueblo's reputed population, but Benavides was known to exaggerate on other matters as when he speaks of Pecos having "more than six thousand houses, six and seven stories high." However, other seventeenth-century references indicated that the Pecos church of Nuestra Señora de los Ángeles de Porciúncula was larger and more resplendent than most. Other documents referred to its having been burned in the 1680 insurrection. The question was raised again in 1956 with publication of the translation of the 1776 description of a New Mexico mission by Fray Francisco Atanásio Domínguez. His accurate, detailed description was obviously of the church which now stands in ruins, but he referred to "an old church outside the wall" to the south. In modern times there was nothing to be seen south of the church but the attached convento. It was partly to resolve the apparent contradictions that Stanley Stubbs of the Museum of New Mexico brought Bruce Ellis and Alfred E. Dittert out to Pecos to excavate a chapel on a separate tongue of the mesa a few hundred yards northeast of the pueblo. What they found was a small church, hardly large enough to have accommodated a hundred bodies at mass. It appeared to have been used only a short time, and had been razed, but not burned. This structure could not have been the magnificent temple of Benavides, nor was it the old church south of the one described in such detail by Domínguez. Pinkley's discovery was unquestionably the footings of the prerebellion mission, and it exonerated Benavides of suspicion of exaggeration. It had, indeed, been a large structure—the largest in New Mexico in its time—and ash and charcoal at the base of the walls were evidence that it had burned.

The year after Pinkley traced the outlines of the old church she was joined by Roland S. Richert from the Park Service's Southwest Archeological Center, who spent the summer of 1968 stabilizing with concrete mortar the old foundation and using adobe to cap and patch the remains of the more recent church. Also in that season, under Pinkley's supervision, tests were made at the south end of the South Pueblo by Hans Lenz, a volunteer. Here, only a few feet north of the churches, Lenz found the bases of thick walls of several un-Indian looking rooms. Although none of them was completely cleared, they were thought to have been secular rooms, temporary quarters for the priest while the permanent church and convento were under construction. Similar rooms had been found at Hawikuh, San Lázaro, and the Pueblo de las Humanas, and were known from documentary sources at San Gabriel.

In February 1969, while planning her final season of field work, Jean Pinkley died leaving to others the work of completing a project she had so ably conducted.

As soon as the weather warmed enough to mix mud and concrete, Richert came back to complete the stabilization work and Alden C. Hayes was assigned to finish the digging, which was accomplished between June and mid-September in 1970.

That summer the rest of the convento was excavated and mapped and a series of trenches and test pits made possible sectional drawings to aid in interpreting the construction sequence. It was established that Domínguez's "old church" south of the last one to be built was a reused section of the convento which was not destroyed with the earlier church. Trenching through a walled compound attached to the cloistered area of the convento led to the discovery of a kiva built by the rebellious Indians who used adobes salvaged from the church they had burned. Also partly excavated that summer were some buildings to the southwest of the convento, thought to be the eighteenth-century "casas reales" referred to by Fray Domínguez. These houses of the king were used by the governor's appointed *alcalde* (mayor) and perhaps by the families of a small garrison that was posted at Pecos from time to time. Other tests a couple of hundred feet farther to the southwest outlined what may have been the remains of a presidio—a large walled courtyard with several small rooms attached. Perhaps this was the "trench" attacked by the Comanches as reported by Governor Vélez in 1751. Another military structure attached to the ruins of the outer east wall of the convento was excavated by Pinkley. This was a D-shaped *torreón* (tower) which, according to local tradition, was

Jean Pinkley and crewman Victor Ortiz inspect the massive buttressed foundation of the newly discovered "first church" during summer, 1967.

used as recently as the early to middle nineteenth century by sentinels watching for hostile Comanches or Apaches.

The nonecclesiastical Spanish structures have only been poked at, and much remains underground, underinvestigated, and unknown. The fascination of Pecos continues.

EPILOGUE • EMIL W. HAURY

Pecos! The word evokes many meanings in the minds of people whose background and interests are different. In the early days, in the rugged and sometimes lawless environment of the West, we learn with some amazement that "to 'pecos a man,' one shot him and rolled his body into the river" (A Dictionary of Americanisms on Historical Principles, 1956). To the Spaniard of the sixteenth century and later, Pecos was a large walled village, the easternmost they had encountered, standing as a kind of gateway between the mountains and the buffalo plains.

For most of us, the meaning of Pecos ranges between the sentimental and the realistic. I am afraid that for the younger set in archeology it is little more than the name of an annual conference, usually held in August, to review the summer's work, few realizing that Pecos was where the original conference was held in 1927. Some of the conclusions then reached still guide our work today. There are those who know Pecos to be a national monument, a place on the map to visit on a vacation tour. But for all those who know the Pecos story in depth, it represents a place where in centuries past many Indian families met the problems of every day living in a stable community, where they dealt with their neighbors, not always on a friendly basis, and where they left for the archeologist to explore what remains of their houses, their kivas, the instructive deposits of trash, the ruins of churches of alien people, even the remains of themselves.

Apart from all that, we think of Pecos as a place where a man had the vision to explore all of these vestiges of another people and time, to break new archeological ground, and deeply enrich the story of the Indians in the Southwest. That man was A. V. Kidder, whose years of study of Pecos left for us a legacy of joining a penetrating and inquiring mental outlook with field archeology, which, I fear, we today are in the process of forgetting. Pecos, of all places in the Southwest, needs to be engraved in our minds as no other, and its hard-learned lessons of putting mind and method together and finally publishing the result in intelligible language should serve as a shining example for the rest of the archeological community to follow.

Kidder saw the story of the American Indian as bearing directly on large issues that troubled him: "What is the relationship between man and his culture?" which is so cogently discussed in his little-known and seldom-read paper called "Looking Backward" (*Proceedings of the American Philosophical Society*, Vol. 83, No. 4, 1940). I am certain that the perils that plagued Pecos from time to time had much to do in framing these questions that so concerned Kidder. It shows that he viewed the excavation of Pecos, although not so stated, as an attempt to understand the larger issues facing man, rather than as an end in itself.

In a way this to me rounds out the work at Pecos, though it shall never be finished, not because investigators have shirked their tasks, but because of the complex human affairs that took place there, and these cannot always be adequately recorded by the archeologist

P*ecos . . . a place where one can reflect on the passage of time and the history of the diverse peoples who saw it as trading partner, mission, landmark, and most of all, home.*

or the historian. There is so much that we cannot hold in our hands or that cannot be put into meaningful perspective until other parts of the equation become known. Bit by bit reconstruction of the whole requires the insight of a number of specialists who must have the interest of the topic at heart, appear on the scene at the right time, and have the craftsmanship to put what they know in words that can be easily understood.

The wide-ranging subject matter in the essays that comprise this volume is a case in point. They represent not only a summation of what we know, but they offer in greater depth matters that could not be fully explored before, and they are testimony that Pecos had more to offer in the way of historical verities than the average archeological site that we know anything about. A part of this is due to Pecos's location, in the eastern limits of what we know as the Southwest and at the threshold of the Great Plains inhabited by a totally different population of Indians. Reactions were bound to follow and they presented a host of intercultural problems nowhere so vividly recorded.

A second and particularly significant factor was the time of Pecos's occupancy. Its heydays spanned the thirteenth and fourteenth centuries in prehistory. Subsequently, the Pecos people experienced the Spanish conquest in a way that was truly matched by no other village. They fell subject to the missionizing efforts of the foreigners, allowing the construction of a pretentious mission and monastery in the Old World idiom; but to show their apprehension of this invasion of a new religion, they were willing participants in the rebellion of 1680 against the alien. Throughout much of this time they had contacts with the Apache, and toward the end of the occupancy of their great village they suffered a devastating conflict with the Comanches, which highlighted the delicate position they were in as a buffer between the sedentist and the nomad. To cap it off, abandonment came in 1838 as a slow and painful finale to the life of the village. Nowhere in the Southwest can we so well read the processes of a village's beginning, its best days, its decline, and death. The thoughtful visitor who stands in the courtyard at Pecos today comes closer to fully appreciating the trials, successes, and failure of a town than is possible elsewhere.

For convenience' sake, we talk about prehistory and history as though a curtain separated them. The date 1540 is usually given as the dividing point because it was then that we have the first written records in the Southwest. When man wrote about his exploits, history began. Pecos illustrates dramatically that this dichotomy is a fiction, for one phase passes imperceptibly into the other. Life before people wrote about it tends to be impersonal, but we are helped enormously when the events were chronicled in detail and responsible personalities were named.

To A. V. Kidder we owe a lasting debt of gratitude for seeing the changes and the chemistry of this long-lived community. He comprehended with amazing insight what happened to the people of Pecos, to the complex architecture, and to the even more puzzling stratigraphy of the accumulated wastage. For the benefit of all those who follow, he left a permanent record of his findings. He pressed hard to understand the sequence of village built on village, the changes in pottery art through time, and the unraveling of the highly instructive, but complicated, refuse left by the living of the sedentary population. Changes in the village structure, in the pottery, and in other aspects of the lives of the Pecos people he saw as the hallmarks of a chronology. He hoped that these were keys that could be used widely throughout the Southwest. He devised the methods to extract the needed information and in his words, he felt that "Pecos may be made to serve as an index to a considerable part of the [Southwestern] culture history, and so, it seems to me, too much effort cannot be spent upon the details of its archeology." While his methodology is useful generally, as it has turned out, the findings at Pecos with respect to pottery kinds and changes in patterns and colors are most directly applicable to the Río Grande Valley. The building of a pan-southwestern pottery chronology was made possible only after the desert and mountain zones far from Pecos were studied, a not surprising development, considering that Kidder's work was done sixty-five to seventy years ago.

But there is another side to the Pecos story that adds to the uniqueness of the ruin. I refer to the interests of the local population that had so much to do with preserving Pecos and the somewhat older Forked Lightning Ruin nearby. Initially, the Gross, Kelly Company protected Pecos from the wasteful and damaging vandalism that so many other ruins in the Southwest have suffered. Kidder found it in almost pristine condition. Largely as a consequence of Kidder's work, Harry W. Kelly and Company donated eighty acres surrounding Pecos, through the Archdiocese of Santa Fe, to the Museum of New Mexico and the School of American Archaeology (now the School of American Research) of Santa Fe for study and preservation. Further, Mr. and Mrs. E. E. Fogelson have assisted the National Park Service enormously by donating 300 acres, including the Forked Lightning Ruin, thereby increasing the area of the monument; and they have generously funded the present-day visitor center and an additional wing to interpret the Mexican and early Anglo periods, so vital in serving the public and in preserving the materials recovered from the ancient village during Kidder's excavations.

The depth of the local interest is best illustrated by the annual procession by the people of the modern town of Pecos to celebrate mass within the standing walls of the old Spanish church, climaxing the Feast of Our Lady of the Angels. At that time a surviving relic from the Pecos mission, in the form of a painting of the patron saint of Pecos, is carried in the procession. The painting was entrusted to the townspeople by the last occupants of Pecos Pueblo when they abandoned the site in 1838. This trust in neighbors and recognition of the treasure the people of the area had in the ruins of Pecos is exemplary. It underscores what an interested and caring public can do in preserving and respecting local antiquities.

Thanks to the curiosity of a restless mind that had, as long ago as 1915, the potential of extracting answers to many interesting and vexing questions, we have the sage of Pecos. Kidder's zeal impelled him to keep his shovel shiny and sharp, for he believed that the answers he sought were to be extracted from the ground. The quality of his uncomplicated writing in telling the story of Pecos, joined with the elaborations by those who came later, in my opinion, reveal what archeology is all about. Thanks, Ted, for blazing the trail so clearly and intelligently for the rest of us to follow.

EMIL W. HAURY

SUGGESTED READINGS

GEOLOGY

de Buys, William, *Enchantment and Exploitation,* University of New Mexico Press, Albuquerque, 1985.

Johnson, R. B., "Pecos National Monument: Its Geologic Setting," *U.S. Geologic Survey Bulletin 1271-5,* 1969.

Sutherland, Patrick K., and Arthur Montgomery, "Trail Guide to the Geology of the Upper Pecos," *Scenic Trips to the Geologic Past,* No. 6, New Mexico Bureau of Mines and Mineral Resources, Socorro, 1981.

EARLY FORAGERS

Irwin-Williams, Cynthia, *The Oshara Tradition: Origins of Anazasi Culture,* Eastern New Mexico University Contributions in Anthropology, Vol. 5, No. 1, Eastern New Mexico University Paleo Indian Institute, Portales, 1973.

Wendorf, Fred and John P. Miller, "Artifacts from High Mountain Sites in the Sangre de Cristo Range, New Mexico," *El Palacio,* Vol. 66, Museum of New Mexico, 1959, pp. 37–52.

Woodbury, Richard B. and Ezra B. W. Zubrow, "Agricultural Beginnings, 2000 B.C.–A.D. 500," in *Handbook of North American Indians,* Vol. 9, Southwest, Smithsonian Institution, Washington, D.C., 1979, pp. 43–60.

EARLY PECOS VALLEY PUEBLOS

Cordell, Linda, "Prehistory: Eastern Anasazi," in *Handbook of North American Indians,* Vol. 9, Southwest, Smithsonian Institution, Washington, D.C., 1979, pp. 131–151.

Kidder, Alfred Vincent, *Pecos, New Mexico: Archaeological Notes,* Papers of the Robert S. Peabody Foundation for Archaeology, Vol. 5, Andover, Mass., 1958.

Wendorf, Fred, and Erik K. Reed, "An Alternative Reconstruction of Northern Rio Grande Prehistory," *El Palacio,* Museum of New Mexico, Vol. 62, 1955, pp. 35–135.

PECOS PUEBLO

Dozier, Edward, *The Pueblo Indians of North America,* Holt, Rinehart and Winston, New York, 1970.

Kidder, Alfred Vincent, *Pecos, New Mexico, Archaeological Notes,* Papers of the Robert S. Peabody Foundation for Archaeology, Vol. 5, Andover, Mass., 1958.

Kidder, Alfred Vincent and Anna O. Shepherd, *The Pottery of Pecos,* Papers of the Phillips Academy Southwestern Expedition, Vol. II, No. 7, New Haven, 1936.

APACHES

Gunnerson, Dolores A., *The Jicarilla Apaches: A Study in Survival,* Northern Illinois University Press, Dekalb, 1974.

Gunnerson, James H., "Southern Athapaskan Archeology," *Handbook of North American Indians,* Vol. 9, Southwest, Smithsonian Insitution, Washington, D.C., 1979, pp. 162–169.

Gunnerson, James H., and Dolores A., "Evidence of Apaches at Pecos," *El Palacio,* Vol. 76, Museum of New Mexico, 1970, pp. 1–6.

SPANISH PERIOD

Bancroft, Hubert Howe, *History of Arizona and New Mexico, 1530–1888,* The History Company, San Francisco, 1889, Horn and Wallace, Albuquerque, 1962.

Benavides, Alonso de, *Fray Alonso de Benavides' Revised Memorial of 1634,* eds., Fredrick Webb Hodge, George P. Hammond, and Agapito Rey, University of New Mexico Press, Albuquerque, 1945.

Hammond, George P., and Agapito Rey, *Narratives of the Coronado Expedition, 1540–1542,* University of New Mexico Press, Albuquerque, 1940.

Kessell, John L., *Kiva, Cross and Crown, The Pecos Indians and New Mexico, 1540–1840,* National Park Service, Washington, D.C., 1979.

Sanchez, Joseph P., *Pueblos, Plains and Province: The New Mexico Frontier 1540–1692*, National Park Service, Unpublished Manuscript, 1986.

Schroeder, Albert H., and Dan S. Matson, eds., *A Colony on the Move: Gaspar Castaño de Sosa's Journal, 1590–1591*, School of American Research, Santa Fe, 1965.

──────── C O M A N C H E S ────────

John, Elizabeth A. H., "Nurturing the Peace: Spanish and Comanche Cooperation in the Early Nineteenth Century," *New Mexico Historical Review*, 59:4, 1984.

John, Elizabeth A. H., *Storms Brewed in Other Men's Worlds: The Confrontation of Indians, Spanish and French in the Southwest 1540–1795*, Texas A & M University Press, College Station, 1975; (paper) University of Nebraska Press, Lincoln, 1981.

Wallace, Ernest, and E. Adamson Hoebel, *The Comanches, Lords of the South Plains*, University of Oklahoma Press, Norman, 1952.

──────── A B A N D O N M E N T ────────

Lange, Charles H., and Carroll J. Riley, eds., *The Southwestern Journals of Adolph F. Bandelier, 1883–1884*, University of New Mexico Press, Albuquerque, 1970.

Schroeder, Albert H., "Pecos Pueblo," *Handbook of North American Indians*, Vol. 9, Southwest, Smithsonian Institution, Washington, D.C., 1979, pp. 430–437.

──────── M E X I C A N P E R I O D ────────

Simmons, Marc, *New Mexico: A Bicentennial History*, W. W. Norton and Company, New York, 1977.

Twitchell, Ralph Emerson, *The Leading Facts of New Mexican History*, Vols. 1 and 2, The Torch Press, Cedar Rapids, 1911–1912, Horn and Wallace, Albuquerque, 1963.

Weber, David J., *The Mexican Frontier, 1821–1846, The American Southwest Under Mexico*, University of New Mexico Press, Albuquerque, 1982.

──────── S A N T A F E T R A I L ────────

Connors, Seymour V., and Jimmy M. Skaggs, *Broadcloth and Britches, The Santa Fe Trade*, Texas A & M University Press, College Station, 1977.

Drumm, Stella M., ed., *Down the Santa Fe Trail and Into Mexico: The Diary of Susan Shelby Magoffin*, University of Nebraska Press, Lincoln, 1982.

Gregg, Josiah, *Commerce of the Prairie*, University of Nebraska Press, Lincoln, 1969.

──────── M E X I C A N W A R ────────

Calvin, Ross, ed., *Lieutenant Emory Reports: A Reprint of Lieutenant W. H. Emory's Notes of a Military Reconnaissance*, University of New Mexico Press, Albuquerque, 1951.

Clarke, Dwight L, *Stephen Watts Kearny, Soldier of the West*, University of Oklahoma Press, Norman, 1961.

Keleher, William A., *Turmoil in New Mexico, 1846–1848*, The Rysal Press, Santa Fe, 1952.

──────── C I V I L W A R ────────

Alberts, Don E., ed., *Rebels on the Rio Grande: The Civil War Journals of A. B. Peticolas*, University of New Mexico Press, Albuquerque, 1984.

Colton, Ray C., *The Civil War in the Western Territories: Arizona, Colorado, New Mexico and Utah*, University of Oklahoma Press, Norman, 1959.

Whitford, William Clarke, *Colorado Volunteers in the Civil War: The New Mexico Campaign in 1862*, The State Historical and Natural History Society, Denver, 1906.

──────── S A N T A F E R A I L W A Y ────────

Bryant, Keith L., Jr., *History of the Atchison, Topeka and Santa Fe Railway*, Macmillan Publishing Company, New York, 1974.

Myrick, David F., *New Mexico's Railroads—An Historical Survey*, Colorado Railroad Museum, Golden, 1970.

Worley, E. D., *Iron Horses of the Santa Fe Trail*, Southwest Railway Historical Society, Dallas, 1965.

— A. V. KIDDER & PECOS —

Kidder, A. V., *An Introduction to the Study of Southwestern Archaeology*, Yale University Press, New Haven, 1962. (Reprint of 1924 First Edition)

Nobel, David Grant, ed., *Pecos Ruins*, Annual Bulletin of the School of American Research, Santa Fe, 1981.

Woodbury, Richard, *Alfred V. Kidder*, Columbia University Press, Cambridge, 1973.

COLONIAL PERIOD ARCHEOLOGY

Adams, Eleanor B., and Fray Angelico Chavez, *The Missions of New Mexico, 1776: A Description by Fray Francisco Atanasio Domínguez with Other Contemporary Documents*, University of New Mexico Press, Albuquerque, 1956, 1976.

Hayes, Alden C., *The Four Churches of Pecos*, University of New Mexico Press, Albuquerque, 1974.

Kubler, George, *The Religious Architecture of New Mexico in the Colonial Period and Since the American Occupation*, University of New Mexico Press, Albuquerque, 1972.

INDEX

A
Alvarado, Hernando de, 46, 48, 49
Amtrak, 117
Anasazi culture, 22, 25, 28, 29, 31
Antelope, 35
Anza, Governor Juan Bautista de, 75, 79
Apache Cañon, Battle of, 110
Apaches in Pecos, 73, 78, 134; in 16th century, 40, 42, 43, 44
Archaeology of Pecos. *See* Burials; Kidder, A.V.; Kivas; Pottery *and individual periods of Pecos history*
Archaic culture, 17–18, 20, 22–23, 25
Armijo, Governor Manuel, 90, 92, 102, 103
Armijo, Juan Cristobal, 96
Army of the West, 102, 103
Atchison, Topeka and Santa Fe railroad, 112, 115, 116, 117

B
Baca, Governor Bartolomé, 88
Bandelier, Adolf, 85
Baptisms, 68, 73
Basketmaker III period, 25
Baylor, Colonel John R., 106
Beans, 25, 26, 32
Becknell, William, 86, 94
Benavides, Fray Alonso de, 63, 129
Bigotes, 48, 49, 50
Biruega, Diego de, 56
Bolton, Herbert Eugene, 8
Buffalo, 42, 43, 78
Building material, 37
Burials, 38, 121, 126

C
Cacique, El, 49, 50
Caddoan speakers, 31, 40
Canby, Colonel Edward, 106, 109
Carvajal, Luis de, 54
Castañeda, Pedro de (chronicler), 48–49, 50, 51, 60
Castaño de Sosa, Gaspar, 54, 55, 56 57, 59, 62
Castro, Fray José de, 68, 89

Chapman, Kenneth M., 118
Chavez, Lieutenant Colonel Manuel, 110
Chihuahua Trail, 97
Chivington, Major John M., 109, 110
Christianity. *See* Franciscan friars in Pecos
Church. *See* Mission church and convento (structures)
Cicuye, 35; Spanish seige of, 56, 57, 58. *See also* Pecos
Civil War, 106, 109, 110, 111
Clans, 35
Clark, William, 10
Coal mines, 115
Coalition Period, 31
Collins, James, 110
Colonial Period, 71; archaeology of, 126, 128, 129, 130, 131. *See also* Spanish in Pecos
Comanches in Pecos, 43, 73, 75, 76, 78, 79, 81, 82, 84, 134
Compromise of 1850, 105
Conquest of Mexico, The (Prescott), 97
Copper, 18, 116
Corbett, John M., 129
Corn, 25, 26, 32
Coronado, Francisco Vasquez de, 8, 40, 48, 49, 51, 60
Cortes, Hernán, 46
Cristóbal de Heredia, Maese de Campo, 55
Crops, 25, 26, 32

D
Deer, 35
Denver & Rio Grande railroad, 112
Diary accounts of Pecos, 89, 96, 97
Dick's Ruin, 29
Dittert, Alfred E., 129
Dogs, 42
Domínguez, Fray Francisco Atánasio, 17, 129, 130
Douglass, A.E., 122

E
E.E. Fogelson Visitor Center, 10
Ecueracapa, Comanche chief, 79
Elk, 35

Ellis, Bruce, 129
Encomienda, 71, 73
Epidemics, 82, 84. *See also* Smallpox
Espejo, Antonio de, 52, 62
Estevan the Moor, 48

F
Farming, 17, 22, 32, 88–90
Ferdon, Edwin N., 128
Field, Matt, 96
Fogelson, Colonel E.E., 8–10, 135. *See also* Garson, Greer (Mrs. E.E. Fogelson)
Food sources, 22, 23, 25
Forked Lightning Ruin, 10, 29, 31, 135
Franciscan friars in Pecos, 42, 52, 70, 73, 89; in 17th century, 60, 62, 63, 65, 66

G
Garson, Greer (Mrs. E.E. Fogelson), 8–10
Geology of Pecos, 14, 17, 18
Glorieta Pass: battles of, 106, 109, 110, 111
Glorieta Mesa and Creek, 14, 17
Glorieta-Pecos corridor, 14, 17
Gold, 18, 49, 50, 116
Gold Rush, 99
Gregg, Josiah, 85, 89, 97
Gross, Kelly Company, 135
Guernsey, Samuel J., 118
Guthe, Carl E., 122

H
Harry W. Kelly and Company, 135
Harvey, Fred, 117, 126
Hawikuh, battle at, 48
Hayes, Alden C., 130
Hearths, 23
Hernández, Domingo, 58
Hewett, Edgar L., 124, 126
Hooton, E.A., 121, 128
Hopi, 38
Horses: importance of, 76, 81
Howard, George T., 102
Hunting, 22, 35
Huntington, Collis P., 112

I
Ice Age, 20
Incas, 46
Indian Detours, 117
Indians of Pecos (Hooton), 121
Intermarriage, Spanish-Indian, 65
Introduction to the Study of Southwestern Archaeology (Kidder), 121
Irrigation, 89, 90

J
James, Thomas, 96
Javier, Maese de Campo Francisco, 66
Jewelry, 23

K
Kearny, General Stephen Watts, 92, 99 102, 103, 105
Kidder, A.V., 8, 37, 38, 132, 134; and pecos excavations, 118, 120, 121, 122, 124
Kivas, 26, 37, 84, 85, 130
Kozlowski, Marton, 97

L
Lamar, Mirabeau B., 92
Land laws, 88
Lead, 18, 116
Lenz, Hans, 130
Life span, 38
"Looking Backward" (Kidder), 132
Lumber industry, 115
Luna y Arrellano, Tristan de, 51

M
Magoffin, James W., 102, 103
Magoffin, Susan, 96, 97
Mapmakers, 46
Manifest Destiny, 100
Martínez, Fray Alonso, 62
Mexican War, 99, 100, 103, 105
Mexico: Pecos under, 86, 88, 89, 90, 92
Military buildings, 130
Military power, 35, 90
Milling tools, 22
Mining, 18, 115, 116–17
Mission church and convento (structures),

63, 126, 128, 129, 130
Mogollon culture, 22
Morlete, Captain Juan, 54, 59
Morley, Sylvanus G., 124
Morris, Earl H., 122

N
Nelson, Nels C., 121
New Mexico: U.S. acquisition of, 100, 102, 103, 105
New Mexico & Southern Pacific railroad, 112, 114
Nieto, Juan Rodríguez, 55
Nusbaum, Jesse L., 121, 126, 129

O
Obregón, Baltazar de, 35
Oñate, Juan de, 62, 63
Ortelius, Abraham, 46
Ortiz, Fray Juan Felipe, 68
Otermín, Governor Antonio, 66

P
Padilla, Father Juan de, 51
Parsons, Elsie Clews, 122
Passenger trains, 117
Pawnee Indians, 43
Pecos: abandonment of, 82, 84, 85; geology of, 14, 17, 18; in 18th century, 68, 70, 71, 73, 75; legends about, 96, 97; significance of, 132, 134, 135; under Mexican rule, 86, 88, 89, 90, 92. *See also* Archaic culture; Franciscan friars in Pecos; Pueblo culture
Pecos, Augustín, 84
Pecos River, 14, 17
Pedrosa, Fray Juan de la, 66
Pérez, Andrés, 55, 57
Pérez, Governor Albino, 90
Pinkley, Jean McQuirt, 126, 129, 130
Pino, Colonel Manuel, 103
Pithouses, 26, 28
Pizarro brothers, 46
Plains Indians, 32, 35, 40
Polk, James Knox, 100; administration of, 103
Popé (Indian leader), 65

Population fluctuations, 29, 88–89
Pottery of Pecos, 25, 28, 35, 38, 44, 121, 122, 135
Prescott, William H., 97
Presidios, 90
Priesthood, archaic, 25. *See also* Religion, native
Pueblo Period, 26, 28, 29, 31; architecture of, 37; peak of, 32, 35, 37, 38
Pueblo Revolt, 42, 65, 66, 68, 71, 82
Pyron, Major Charles L., 109, 110

Q
Quitaro, Nicholas, 103
Quivira, 42, 49, 50, 51

R
Railroad, 97; Santa Fe Railway, 112, 114, 115, 116, 117
Reagan, Ronald, 10
Reisner, G.A., 118
Religion, native, 32, 35, 84, 134
Religious articles, 17, 23
Reservations, 81
Richert, Roland S., 130
Rocks and minerals, 17–18
Rowe Ruin, 29

S
700 Pueblo, 38
Salazar, Martín de, 56
San Miguel, Fray Francisco de, 63
San Miguel village, 75, 84, 88, 89
Sánchez, Francisco Chamuscado, 52, 62
Sandia Mountain campaign, 73
Santa Ana, Antonio Lopez, 90
Santa Fe: Pueblo seige of, 66.
Santa Fe Trail, 84, 88; epic of, 94, 96, 97, 99
Scurry, Lieutenant Colonel William R., 109, 110, 111
Shepard, Anna O., 122
Sibley, General Henry, 106, 109
Sibley's Brigade, 106, 109
Silver, 18, 97, 99, 117
Slave trade, 42, 54

Slough, Colonel John P., 109, 110
Smallpox, 75, 81, 82
South Pueblo, 38
Southern Pacific railroad, 112
Spanish in Pecos, 35, 38, 52, 54; first arrival of, 46, 48, 49, 50, 51; recapture New Mexico, 68, 70, 71, 73, 75; revolts against, 65, 66. *See also* Franciscan friars in Pecos
Squash, 25, 26, 32
Stagecoaches, 97
Stone artifacts, 44
Storage pit, 28
Stubbs, Stanley, 129
Suárez, Fray Andrés, 63

T
Taylor, Zachary, 103
Tecolote Range, 14, 17
Tello, Fray Antonio, 60
Texas, 90, 92, 105
Texas Rangers. *See* Silbley's Brigade
Tiguex War, 50
Tipi-ring site, 43
Tools, 17, 22, 28, 37
Tourist trade, 117
Trade, 14, 35, 40, 42, 43, 81, 88
Trash mounds, 128
Treaty of Guadalupe Hidalgo, 103
Tree-ring dating, 122
Túpatu, Luis, 68
Turco, El, 49, 50, 51

U
Úbeda, Fray Luis de, 51, 60, 62, 66
Unrest/unsettlement, periods of, 29, 31

V
Vaca, Cabeza de, 48
Valliant, Susan, 126, 129
Vargas, Governor Don Diego de, 68, 70, 73
Velasco, Fray Fernando de, 60, 66
Velasco, Viceroy Luis de, 54, 59
Vélez Cachupín, Governor Tomás, 73, 78, 79
Vetancourt, Augustín de (chronicler), 63
Vigil y Alarid, Governor Juan Bautista, 103

Villamanrique, Viceroy Marqués de, 54

W
Water, 17, 29
Weapons, 17, 22, 25
Weaving, 35, 37
Willey, Gordon, 121
Witkind, William Boris, 128, 129
Women, 22, 81

Y
Ysopete, 50, 51

Z
Zeinos, Fray Diego de, 73
Zia, 38
Zinc, 18, 116
Zubiría y Escalante, Bishop José Antonio Laureano, 89
Zuni Indians, 38, 48

ACKNOWLEDGMENTS

The editors and the National Park Service wish to express their gratitude to the following individuals and organizations, whose generosity made this volume possible.

Mrs. Greer Garson Fogelson
The Conrad N. Hilton Foundation
Banquest/First National Bank of Santa Fe
The Friends of Pecos National Monument
Mrs. Charles Vychopen
Mr. Larry Wilson and Ms. Mary Post
Daughters of the American Revolution, Stephen Watts Kearny Chapter
Sons of Confederate Veterans, General William R. Scurry Camp 1385
Public Service Company of New Mexico
Village of Pecos
Mr. Dean Weldon
New Mexico Federal Savings and Loan Association, Albuquerque
Embassy of Spain
Consulado General de España
Mr. John S. Catron
New Mexico Federal Savings and Loan Association, Santa Fe
Historical Society of New Mexico
United Daughters of the Confederacy, New Mexico Division
The Glorieta Baptist Conference Center
Mr. Roy and Mrs. Louann Ihde Andersen
Ms. Darlene M. Trujillo

Our appreciation is also extended to Ms. Darlene M. Trujillo, Ms. Mary Macaulay, and Ms. Amanda Friedman for a splendid job of reviewing the manuscript. We are indebted to the authors of the volume and the other following reviewers for their suggestions and constructive criticism: Arthur Trevena, Tom Edrington, Don Alberts, Robert Lister, Milford Fletcher, Richard Chapman, David Myrich, Curtis Schaafsma, Les McFadden, Paul Karas, and David Brugge.

THE WHITE HOUSE

WASHINGTON

February 19, 1988

I am pleased and proud to add a few words to this
volume about Pecos National Monument. This work will
tell Americans and visitors to our land a great deal
about the fascinating history and heritage of the Pecos
area, the American Southwest, and the Great Plains.

That is good news for all of us, because it means that
succeeding generations will learn the story of the many
peoples over the centuries who lived in and traversed
the magnificent crossroads of a continent that is the
Pecos. American Indians, Spaniards, Mexicans, trappers,
traders, troopers, scouts, soldiers, cowmen, and countless
others have all peopled the Pecos and left their imprint
on the land -- and on the heart of America.

This trove of fact and lore is brought closer to us by
this volume -- and by the vision, the public spirit, and
the determination of the late Colonel Buddy Fogelson
and his wife Greer Garson Fogelson, who helped make
the Pecos National Monument a reality and a lasting
legacy. May everyone who contemplates the Pecos and
its rich meaning do so in their spirit and in the spirit
of this volume.

Ronald Reagan